Help! My Students Write Like They Text

Help! My Students Write Like They Text

Teaching Code-Switching to Improve Writing

Jennifer French

ROWMAN & LITTLEFIELD
Lanham • Boulder • New York • London

Published by Rowman & Littlefield
An imprint of The Rowman & Littlefield Publishing Group, Inc.
4501 Forbes Boulevard, Suite 200, Lanham, Maryland 20706
www.rowman.com

Unit A, Whitacre Mews, 26-34 Stannary Street, London SE11 4AB

Copyright © 2018 by Jennifer French

All rights reserved. No part of this book may be reproduced in any form or by any electronic or mechanical means, including information storage and retrieval systems, without written permission from the publisher, except by a reviewer who may quote passages in a review.

British Library Cataloguing in Publication Information Available

Library of Congress Cataloging-in-Publication Data

Names: French, Jennifer, 1979- author.
Title: Help! my students write like they text : teaching code-switching to improve writing / Jennifer French.
Description: Lanham, Maryland : Rowman & Littlefield, [2018] | Includes bibliographical references.
Identifiers: LCCN 2018012524 (print) | LCCN 2018028088 (ebook) | ISBN 9781475839463 (electronic) | ISBN 9781475839449 (cloth : alk. paper) | ISBN 9781475839456 (pbk. : alk. paper)
Subjects: LCSH: Language arts (Secondary) | English language—Composition and exercises—Study and teaching (Secondary) | Text messages (Cell phone systems) | Code switching (Linguistics)
Classification: LCC LB1631 (ebook) | LCC LB1631 .F696 2018 (print) | DDC 428.0071/2—dc23
LC record available at https://lccn.loc.gov/2018012524

∞ ™ The paper used in this publication meets the minimum requirements of American National Standard for Information Sciences Permanence of Paper for Printed Library Materials, ANSI/NISO Z39.48-1992.

Printed in the United States of America

Trent, because of you I can make my dreams possible. Samuel, Nathan, Hannah, and Jackson: You're the reason education matters <3

Contents

Foreword		ix
Acknowledgments		xi
Introduction		xiii
1	It's All about Efficiency	1
2	"The Effects"	11
3	Changing Perspectives	21
4	Flipping the Switch	33
5	Classroom Practice	41
Research Study		59
Textspeak Glossary		75
References		83
About the Author		89

Foreword

Jennifer French, a forward-thinking and inspired educator, is never afraid of a challenge—and researching the effect of texting on student writing is definitely not an easy task.

I met Dr. French when I was brought in as a consultant to Anderson Public Schools, Indiana. At that time, she had already begun questioning how the act of texting affected student writing. Like most of our colleagues, she and I assumed that the effect was mostly negative. How could short bursts of two-thumbed keyboarding, resulting in messages consisting largely of abbreviations and acronyms, help student writers learn to craft sentences, let alone paragraphs? But as Dr. French's research progressed, she realized that she had to rethink these assumptions. It turns out that writing, specifically in English, is a malleable skill that can be positively influenced by many unexpected variables, including texting.

The fact is many of us now walk around with powerful computers in our pockets. The speed at which we can gather, digest, and share information is truly mind-boggling. As French points out in her opening chapter, contemporary language development simply reflects this momentum and efficiency. Today's students are as comfortable with search engines as my generation was with the now-archaic card catalogue. The beauty of living language is that it reflects the changes in a society and culture. Textspeak, with all of its quirky abbreviations and acronyms, has become commonplace. Even though words and phrases like "SMS" and "LOL" are already in the dictionary, teachers can't help but fear they're witnessing the death of Standard English.

But fear not, good teachers! Dr. French is an educator to the core, and as such she is happy to share her newfound discoveries and keen insights about texting and its effects on student writing. In her opening chapter, she explains the dynamic attributes of language and how they affect our students. As

French points out, it is essential that literacy instructors embrace this notion. To be truly responsive educators, we must accept that the demands of language now include texting.

The author furthers her exploration in chapter 2, where she focuses on different types of learners, including English language learners. She continues in chapters 3 and 4 by considering the essential skill of "code switching." That's the skill that allows us to transition back and forth between formal and casual language and recognize the appropriate contexts and settings for each. She concludes in chapter 5 by sharing concrete classroom activities and comprehension strategies that will help students recognize and navigate various contexts and settings.

Indeed, the most valuable aspect of Dr. French's book is her ability to translate her research into practice. Much of this book is dedicated to providing teachers with *real* solutions, instructional ideas, and lessons that embrace texting. Our students' use of texting can and should be used to liberate and empower writing skill development. Dr. French has shown us how to do so in this excellent resource for educators.

Katherine S. McKnight, PhD
Founder, EngagingLearners.com

Acknowledgments

I would like to thank all of my colleagues and friends for their willingness to try something new.

I'd also like to acknowledge Dr. Katie McKnight, a personal mentor and a beloved friend. She has made me a better teacher and a stronger woman.

Introduction

IMHO, LOL, OIC, OMG. If you've recently graded middle school or high school writing, chances are you've read terms like these; or my favorite, "wtf – idk," which also happened to be an answer on a student's quiz. As a middle school English teacher, I became more and more perplexed to see students using texting talk on their homework and classroom writing assignments—not to mention answers on the writing portion of the state standardized test. My students were not differentiating appropriate writing contexts. The answers written on the unit test were written the same way that they invited their friends to "hang @ *$" (Starbucks).

It was 2005, and almost every one of my 140 eighth-graders had their own cell phone; much of the time it was a model newer than mine. In my school district, the majority of discipline referrals between 2006 and 2008 were written because of student cell phone misuse. The clever students were able to text answers to a student in another class by blindly texting from their hoodie pockets. Students who could escape teacher view would take a photo of someone else's completed work to copy later. Sneakiness had a new platform. Confiscating cell phones meant calls l8r (later) from angry parents. My colleagues and I were fighting a losing battle, and our students were ROFL (rolling on floor, laughing).

The greatest challenge from cell phones was the birth of textspeak. Textspeak relies on shortcuts by utilizing acronyms, shortened misspellings, and the avoidance of grammar. It was everywhere. It was the first decade of the twenty-first century, and the textspeak plague was spreading. Teachers were complaining to administrators, and parents were complaining to teachers. Textspeak was quickly corroding English language. Thus, I began my quest to save Standard English from the clutches of middle schoolers. As my journey began, I was certain of what I would find: high doses of texting directly correlating to lower writing grades and test scores.

What I found, however, was not what I had expected. Research demonstrates that younger students who utilized textspeak actually performed *better* in areas of literacy. Students must have phonological awareness and understanding to manipulate language as textspeak requires. Likewise, the research on adolescent writing had not proven detrimental; by the time undergraduate students reach college, they *typically* have mastered contextual writing and have learned when *not* to use textspeak or slang.

The answers that I wanted to find through this research are very different from the results I actually found. However, it has deepened my understanding of culture, language, and my students, and I treasure each one more because of it. It's my hope that exploring this information will have the same effect on the readers and that they will deepen their understanding of spoken and written language.

Chances are that you've gravitated toward this book because you are currently dealing with a similar issue in your classroom. You are not alone. Across the United States, middle school and high school teachers are simultaneously banging their heads on whiteboards. They are frustrated by lack of capitalization and punctuation, and with each missing vowel, their discouragement grows.

Colleague and high school teacher John Lotz explains that "the vernacular they [high school students] use so commonly in their daily social interactions has become so ingrained that they're not even aware of how they speak or write. In theory, they understand that they're supposed to take their audience into consideration; however, in practice, they often say things that are completely inappropriate, not to mention lol, lmao, lmfao, wtf, rofl, and even emojis in some of their formal essays and journals. It is somewhat entertaining, albeit painful, to see the new and creative ways some of our students have learned to butcher the language!"

Middle school technology teacher Maria Sellers's feelings toward textspeak: "In all reality, someone has been super creative along the way. A new language, although unacademic, has been created and implemented. The creator has created a symbolic language coupled with phonetics. Unfortunately, this creation is not appropriate in academia. Even more unfortunate is students' lack of understanding surrounding those ever so important usage boundaries."

Yet there is hope for our celebrated language and optimism for our moldable students. The answer, however, may be one that you aren't quite ready to accept. The remedy isn't in a new and improved cell phone school policy, screen surveillance software, or reinstitution of spelling curriculum. It's in the adjustment of educator attitudes and our understanding of the evolution of language. It's in our acceptance of our students—their needs and interests.

When students feel that both the teacher and the classroom work are relevant, they will be apt to engage.

My first lesson was to understand language through a cultural lens. Speaking is a primary language, whereas writing is a secondary language, and the acquisition of both depends on the culture of the individual. Lev Vygotsky explains that children learn as a social activity and that those activities are determined by the child's environment. The child internalizes the behavior so that he can assimilate to his culture. Texting is a method of communicating with others for a social purpose through a practice that is learned within one's culture. It's a shared language. The more submerged in the texting experience, the more one learns, internalizes, and uses (Ormrod, 2011).

A common teaching practice for students who are learning English is to allow them to think and initially respond in their primary language. Once their initial thoughts have been processed, they work to translate the information to their secondary language. Similarly, students may need to think and respond in the language with which they are most comfortable, *even* if that language is textspeak. Once the learner's thoughts have been recorded, the practice of rewriting, or translanguaging, can follow. Some students may need to practice this process for the entirety of their education, but this will vary from learner to learner.

How do we as educators and parents allow students to creatively express themselves, support them academically, and prepare them for a professional world built on written and verbal communication? Herein lies this text. Hopefully, it will alleviate the concerns of those who are worried about the disintegration of the English language and help those ISO (in search of) strategies to support textspeaking learners.

Chapter One

It's All about Efficiency

Gone is the skill of composing lengthy correspondence. Today, the key is brevity (and, seemingly, the ability to communicate in 140 characters or less). A rapidly evolving and tech-based world has led to the adaptation of a more efficient language: textspeak. *Textspeak*, now its own genre of language, consists of abbreviations, acronyms, symbols, word adaptations, slang, and the lack of grammar. Also known as textese, textism, or digi-talk, it is rooted in Standard English, but it is actually more reflective of colloquial spoken language. It is an interactive form of communication that takes place through electronic technologies, such as text messaging, email, and instant messaging.

The once-limited devices of early technology birthed a need for a quicker way to communicate—a necessary shortcut—a few of the more popular shortcuts being brb, be right back; ttyl, talk to you later; and lol, laugh out loud. Another integral component of textspeak is emojis, those graphics depicting various emotions that are used to express feelings rather than writing a reaction.

Like a rapidly spreading disease, textspeak has touched every continent. Studies on texting have been conducted by researchers in Pakistan, Canada, England, Germany, and Africa as well as across the United States. Textspeak has reached every social level: friends, family, colleagues, and even the political world.

Those most affected by far are American adolescents. Kids between the ages of thirteen and seventeen send an average of 3,364 text messages each month, which is more than any other age group (Cingel & Sundar, 2012). This doubles the number of text messages sent by eighteen- to twenty-four-year-olds, which is 1,640. Text messaging is becoming the most preferred method of communication, as exhibited by the 200,000 text messages sent per second across the globe (Grace, Kemp, Martin, & Parrila, 2013).

Textspeak is not limited to a few localized, quirky acronyms; sociolinguistics accept textspeak as its own genre of reading and writing. The texting language has become so ubiquitous that phrases are being included in dictionaries as an accepted word in the English language. Text dictionaries, which translate textspeak into Standard English, are now common tools found online *and* in bookstores. The pervasiveness of texting among adolescents has even earned the term "youth code" because it is the primary language of America's modern youth (Durken, Conti-Ramsden, & Walker, 2011).

It's not just text messaging. In a study by Common Sense Media (Rideout, 2012), titled "Children, Teens, and Entertainment Media: The View from the Classroom," it is noted that children and teens spend more time with media in general—like listening to music and watching television, interacting with social media, and playing video games—more than any other activity besides sleeping, often using several modes of media simultaneously! This amount has doubled during the decade between 1999 and 2009.

Children between the ages of eight and eighteen spend more than 7.5 hours a day interacting with media, which is more time than they spend in school. Even children between the ages of five and eight spend 168 hours a year more with media than with school (Rideout, 2012). Parents are often a catalyst of this phenomenon, and a significant number are reported to download apps for keeping their children occupied in the car or while running errands (Lenhart, Arafeh, Smith, & Macgill, 2008).

It is no wonder that this generation has earned the title "Digital Natives." They are the first generation to be fluent in the language that rules computers, video games, and the Internet (Prensky, 2001). Digital language is the primary way in which adolescents communicate; so it is reasonable to assume that it shows up in their academic work (Lewin, 2008). This is an assumption that has both teachers and parents worried (Cingel & Sundar, 2012).

In fact, 71 percent of teachers fear that technology's effect has negatively affected students academically—specifically, their attention span and writing skills. Eighty-one percent of middle school teachers believe that texting has the most negative influence on student achievement, especially the writing portion of standardized tests (Rideout, 2012).

One teacher stated, "Students now write papers like they are texting and do not really consider grammar and spelling before turning in compositions" (Rideout, 2012, p. 26). It is also assumed that the brevity of texting and online chatting has influenced writing stamina in the classroom with a student's abilities to write an extensive composition. Teachers complain about students groaning when a writing composition has a required length of two or more pages. Beyond teachers and parents, other child advocates are raising concerns about the quality of communication and writing that American students produce (Hawley Turner & Hicks, 2011).

Danesi (2009) conducted an investigation to find the reason behind the changing English language system. After reviewing the current trends of change in cyberlanguage, he applied the *principle of least effort*. This principle states that all language evolves with the purpose of efficiency in communication. Textspeak is a product of striving for a more simplistic form of communication brought on by the invention of cellular telephone messaging. The principle of least effort provides a framework for understanding the origination of textspeak.

Textspeak omits grammar and punctuation and uses acronyms and simplistic spelling. It creates a more concise language, which is more efficient when keying the words on a mobile device. When texting first began, each key was pressed several times to retrieve the needed alphabet letter. As technology has advanced, tools such as autocorrect will assume the word the author is writing and complete the spelling. Also coined the "lazy language," textspeak points to the goal of efficiency, which simplifies spelling, as the factor, therefore altering written language.

Everyone is a new language learner, despite cultural demographics, age, or situation. Humans are constantly learning new words, phrases, and terminology and being exposed to new dialects or accents. Essentially, textspeak is a new and acceptable language constructed by its authors to meet their communication needs. This may be heartbreaking news for the classroom teacher. (I know my high school English teacher would roll over in her grave if she thought a lowercase "i" had become an acceptable practice in English language.) However, textspeak isn't any different from other practices that have created an efficiency in communication.

NOTHING NEW

Although the textism phrases are now widely recognized, they are not new inventions. Think of the telegraph. This was a turning point historically for communication. The system was created in the 1840s by Samuel Morse, who developed the system for transmitting electrical signals using a code he developed by assigning dots and dashes to each letter of the alphabet. When communication is costly or cumbersome, abbreviations are necessary, and Morse Code is a prime historical example (Mackenzie-Hoy, 2006, p. 1).

Stenography, or shorthand, was also invented to expedite communication. Stenography uses the same approach to communication as texting: symbols and abbreviations. Furthermore, stenography is based on phonetic spelling! Shorthand dates back to ancient Greece but became most widely used around 63 BCE in the Roman Empire.

Over thousands of years, versions of shorthand have come and gone and been translated into almost every language. In 1837, an educator by the name of Sir Isaac Pitman developed the most widely used shorthand system based on omitting vowels—the same strategy used in textspeak. Stenography continued to evolve, and in 1893 *schools began teaching shorthand to students as a necessary business skill* (Shorthand, n.d.). Later, shorthand was adapted as a system for typewriter use. Sixty rules are applied to abbreviate more than 20,000 words. Comparably, there are 227 pages in the "online textlingo dictionary" listing the most commonly used textspeak abbreviations.

In 1906, a Stenograph machine was invented and used to aid court reporters. A Stenotype machine was also invented and used to record speech. "Both machines have keyboards of 22 keys. Because the operator uses all fingers and both thumbs, any number of keys can be struck simultaneously" (Shorthand, n.d.). Hmmm, that sounds familiar. Text messaging employs both elements used by these machines: typing with multiple fingers and thumbs and mimicking a voice-to-text feature.

In 1985, a member of the Global System for Mobile Communication (GSM) by the name of Friedhelm Hillebrand wanted to develop a text messaging system to use with the car phone. The limited bandwidth would allow for only short messages (Milian, 2009). After experimenting, he found that most messages could be effectively communicated in 160 characters per message, which was similar to the length of a standard postcard.

Various connections can be made between shorthand and texting. Nearly three hundred research studies have been done on the reading and writing of shorthand. The results indicate that "Good readers of shorthand were also good readers of print" (Anderson, 1981, p. 75, para. 3) and habits that were formed early during the learning of shorthand persisted throughout the course of using it (Anderson, 1981). One study (Bloom, 2010) found that there was an increase in the reading ability of children when they began texting, which illustrates that an individual must have a solid understanding of language to use an unconventional form of it and if there is no solid foundation of language, bad habits may be hard to break.

VOICE

Beyond the convenience of a more efficient communication, researchers may have discovered another motive for utilizing textspeak: expression of emotion. Up to 70 percent of communication can be nonverbal (Adler & Proctor, 2014). When communicating electronically, it is more difficult to express tone, attitude, or emotion. Just like we hear emotion in someone's voice during a phone call, we hear the author's voice in written communication.

As educators, we tirelessly teach students to identify the speaker's tone and the author's purpose in a text (major components in the Common Core Career and Readiness Standards). Similar to identifying the speaker's tone, the tone or attitude identified in the voice of a text or an email is known as *virtual body language*.

Textisms and emoticons can aid in providing this missing piece in dialogue. For instance, "lol" substitutes what would typically be communicated in person through voice or gesture. This could lead us to believe that the use of text language is not because of grammatical ignorance or literacy weakness but rather is a desire to express one's electronic correspondence more articulately.

For example, a question followed by three question marks illustrates the author's confusion or emphasizes the need for clarification. Wouldn't you agree??? Emoticons can prop up our conversation and help the reader determine tone. One challenge, however, is that unlike a phone conversation where emotion can be heard, emojis have the power to send a message the author is trying to convey even though her heart isn't in it. It can even be passive-aggressive to make a statement that is controversial or argumentative and follow it with a smiley face ("You're not wearing that outfit again, are you :-)").

Educators, students who utilize textspeak aren't warring a personal attack on the language that you hold most dear. Instead of viewing textspeak as a detriment to the English language, understand that it is a natural evolution of written communication. It is an acceptable and social practice.

Our job is to teach the appropriate utilization and further students' understanding of language in context. It's not necessary to know all the latest terms in textspeak. What's important is that educators are open to the possibilities of translanguaging and the depth of learning that various codes can bring to a classroom.

EVOLUTION

Unlike linguists, educators have been slow to understand that changes in language are expected. Regard the excerpt from Guy Deutscher's *The Unfolding of Language: An Evolutionary Tour of Mankind's Greatest Invention*:

> I take it you already know
> Of tough and bough and cough and dough?
> Others may stumble, but not you,
> On hiccough, thorough, lough and through?
> Well done! And now you wish, perhaps,
> To learn of less familiar traps?
> Beware of heard, a dreadful word
> That looks like beard and sounds like bird,

> And dead: it's said like bed, not bead —
> For goodness sake don't call it deed!
> Watch out for meat and great and threat
> (They rhyme with suite and straight and debt).
> A moth is not a moth in mother,
> Nor both in bother, broth in brother,
> And here is not a match for there
> Nor dear and fear for bear and pear,
> And then there's dose and rose and lose —
> Just look them up—and goose and choose,
> And cork and work and card and ward,
> And font and front and word and sword,
> And do and go and thwart and cart —
> Come, come, I've hardly made a start!
> A dreadful language? Man alive!
> I'd mastered it when I was five!

Language is in constant evolution—a process of trial and error. Regardless of age and background, everyone is a language learner. Everyone continues to acquire vocabulary whether it's within a new social group or when one experiences a new geographic dialect.

If you frequent Starbucks, you have adapted a specific vocabulary for that context. You will most likely request a *tall* chai tea sweetened, instead of a *small*. During a recent visit to a fast-food establishment, my eleven-year-old son ordered his meal with "no Arby's sauce." He looked hurt when the ladies behind the counter laughed at him and assured him that it wouldn't be a problem. I had to remind him, "Honey, this is Wendy's." This event demonstrated to him that context is important and that, although vocabulary may be appropriate in one situation, it may not be in a different—*although similar*—setting.

Embrace the changes that evolve in language, and expand curriculum to explore the hidden rules and structure of the *informal* English language that has always existed but has never been validated. Shirley Brice Heath's (1999) work, *Ways with Words: Language, Life, and Work in Communities and Classrooms*, is an extended ethnographic study that explores the effect of culture on language development and its influence on communication problems in school and work. Heath asserts that all professional and social discourse is steeped in personal culture. The ability to identify and learn the hidden rules of language will determine an individual's success in the world. This work extends to the use of textspeak as one mode of cultural discourse, birthed out of modern culture, shared between peer groups, and inadvertently blended into all other discourse.

Vygotsky's social cognitive theory describes how children learn as a social activity and those activities are determined by the child's environment. An individual learns from his environment and then internalizes the behavior for the purpose of assimilating to his culture (Ormrod, 2011). In this case, the theory supports that texting is a method of communicating with others for a social purpose by utilizing a practice that is learned within one's culture.

Texting is a social experience. The more submerged in the texting experience, the more one will learn new words and phrases. It is a shared language among a similar culture. Most educators use the social cognitive theory to support the strategy of small-group instruction; however, it encompasses more than just collaborative learning. Even when an individual is alone, her thinking involves others, and her thoughts are cultivated by her surroundings both in content and execution (Smagorinsky, 2007).

Vygotsky's 1930 work, *Mind and Society*, examines the prehistory of written language:

> Unlike the teaching of spoken language, into which children grow of their own accord, the teaching of written language is based on artificial training. Such training requires an enormous amount of attention and effort on the part of teacher and pupil and thus becomes something self-contained, relegating living written language to the background. Instead of being founded on the needs of children as they naturally develop and on their own activity, writing is given to them from without, from the teacher's hands. This situation recalls the development of a technical skill such as piano-playing: the pupil develops finger dexterity and learns to strike the keys while reading music, but he is no way involved in the essence of the music itself. . . . A second conclusion, then, is that writing should be meaningful for children, that an intrinsic need should be aroused in them, and that writing should be incorporated into a task that is necessary and relevant for life. Only then can we be certain that it will develop not as a matter of hand and finger habits but as a really new and complex form of speech. (p. 15)

Writing has been traditionally taught as an outside force. Students are often asked to write in response to artificial situations, where they may have difficulty engaging with the assignment or task, instead of approaching the teaching of writing similarly to language acquisition, which is based on need and interest. For example, a writing assessment for seventh-graders asked students to imagine they were a jarred pickle and write about their life story. This task requires students to demonstrate their writing proficiency by examining a process with which they have no association, connection, or engagement. If we're asking for evidence of a student's ability to demonstrate understanding of a process or his ability to write creatively, then a better approach would be to ask him to write about a process he experiences daily.

Jean Piaget developed schema theory, which examines how new ideas are connected to current thinking. This is especially relevant to language development. The purpose of textspeak is to communicate more efficiently. In textspeak, words that may take ten letters to spell (current knowledge) must be abbreviated with a symbol or only a few letters to communicate the same meaning (new knowledge). By the time a student reaches adolescence, she should have learned traditional spelling and writing structure through her elementary education. For most, the knowledge of spelling and writing structure was formed prior to adopting textspeak.

Acquiring textspeak can broaden an individual's language experience (Ormrod, 2011). If an adolescent begins utilizing textspeak before having a concrete understanding of standard English, it will all be categorized as new knowledge. Students could easily retrieve either information in a writing task and find it difficult to differentiate the appropriate form. Students who are writing in an academic setting may struggle with writing in context and whether to use Standard English or textspeak. Therein lies the danger. Because we can't control a student's exposure to various forms of language, our responsibility rests on helping him to determine the context for each.

However, the popular assumption that digital language is causing the English language to deteriorate is unfounded. Andrea Lunsford, from Stanford University, collected nearly nine hundred college freshman compositions from 1917 to 2006. She analyzed the rate of errors in each composition and anticipated an increase of writing mistakes in spelling, grammar, and word use. After nearly one hundred years, the rate of errors hadn't increased.

Furthermore, compositions had increased in length from an average of 162 words in 1917 to an average of 1,038 in 2006. The writing was also found to be much more complex, taking on argumentative and research styles as compared to the common expository format of the early 1900s. Professor Lunsford explains that writing in an online environment provides a sense of purpose for students that the classroom doesn't provide. Students are likely to write 40 percent more for a real audience, with better organization and content (Fishman, Lunsford, McGregor, & Otuteye, 2005).

KEY POINTS

- *Textspeak*, now its own genre of language, consists of abbreviations, acronyms, symbols, word adaptations, slang, and the lack of grammar.
- Eighty-one percent of middle school teachers believe that texting has the most negative influence on student achievement, especially the writing portion of standardized tests.
- Everyone is a new language learner, despite cultural demographics, age, or situation. Humans are constantly learning new words, phrases, and terminology and being exposed to new dialects or accents.
- Stenography uses the same approach to communication as texting: symbols and abbreviations.

- There is an increase in the reading ability of children when they begin texting, illustrating that an individual must have a solid understanding of language to use an unconventional form of it.
- Similar to identifying the speaker's tone, the tone or attitude identified in the voice of a text or an email is known as *virtual body language*. Textisms and emoticons can aid in providing this missing piece in dialogue.
- Our job as teachers is to teach the appropriate utilization and further students' understanding of language in context. It's not necessary to know all the latest terms in textspeak. What's important is that educators be open to the possibilities of translanguaging and the depth of learning it can bring to a classroom.

Chapter Two

"The Effects"

COLLEGE STUDENTS

The bulk of research conducted on the relationship between literacy and texting has been done at the university level. Undergraduate students make easy test subjects. They are no longer minors, and they're easily accessible to university researchers who are prowling for participants.

Past studies have discovered that US (and foreign) college students, ages eighteen to twenty-five, know when to utilize textspeak. For instance, undergraduate students will use textspeak in social formats but will refrain from using texting language in professional or academic settings (Drouin, 2011).

This demonstrates that the use of textism for a college student is a conscious effort. Contrary to belief, "it does not appear that textese just seeps out into writing everywhere and in equal amounts" (Drouin, 2011, p. 72). In one study, undergraduate students applied textisms in their writing 13 to 16 percent of the time. More specifically, the textisms used by college students are primarily missing capitalization and punctuation, not spelling (Grace et al., 2013).

Another study found that the adults who had difficulty learning to read as children use more textese when sending text messages (Grace et al., 2013). The assumption is that students who struggled to learn to read also experienced lower levels of literacy confidence while forming views about the value of conventional spelling, which lead to greater psychosocial freedom to use textisms as adults.

Researchers also suggest that the college students who use Standard English instead of textspeak view texting as immature. Other factors that may influence the results are phone model capability, length of cell phone ownership, and social pressures (Plester, Wood, & Bell, 2008). Undergraduates' fluency of textism is not negatively associated with students' Standard English writing skills. Furthermore, spelling and writing skills are not hindered by exposure to textspeak because, by the time students are in college, they have a solid foundation of language structure and are not as easily influenced by the bombardment of textisms (Powell & Dixon, 2011).

Employing textisms in one's electronic correspondence may be considered a rite of passage for adolescents. Ability to speak fluent textese may proudly display an adolescent's connection to her culture and prominent use of the latest technology devices. Using textspeak affords the opportunity for students to experience a positive identification with their peers, and although displaying one's fluency in textspeak may be positive for younger generations, it has reverse effects for the adults. Educated or professional adults strive to embody an image of maturity and expertise and often avoid use of textisms, symbols, and emoticons so that they don't appear immature or unprofessional (Lewis & Fabos, 2005).

EFFECTS ON CHILDREN

Research displays mixed results of the effect of texting on children. Fewer studies have been done on the age group of ten- to twelve-year-olds. In 2008, 19 percent of eight- to eleven-year-olds and 76 percent of twelve- to fourteen-year-old children owned a personal cell phone (Kemp & Bushnell, 2011). The average age for children to receive their first cell phone is ten years old (Cingel & Sundar, 2012).

It was also found that children ages six and seven could link an increase in their reading ability to when they began texting (Bloom, 2010). The ability to use abbreviations and symbols for words requires the knowledge of linguistic rules. An individual must have a solid understanding of language to create and use an unconventional form of it.

In a study done by Coe and Oakhill (2011), English and Australian children consistently exhibited positive links to literacy and texting behaviors. Their plausible explanation is that texting displays an awareness of linguistic principles, such as phonetic spelling, friendly pronunciations, and nonverbal codes. In *Txting: The gr8 db8*, Crystal (2008) examines the effects text messaging has on literacy in eleven languages: English, French, Spanish, Italian, German, Swedish, Finnish, Welsh, Dutch, Chinese, and Portuguese. All were said to be positively affected by texting.

Children between ten and eleven years old who sent three or more text messages a day had considerably lower literacy scores than children who sent less than three messages a day (Plester, Wood, & Joshi, 2009). Conflicting studies by Plester, Wood, & Joshi (2009) show children who are strong at text translation activities and who have a higher use of textisms per message score better in spelling, reading, writing, phonological awareness, and vocabulary.

Plester et al. (2008) looked at eleven-year-old students and established that children who have high text density (Rosen, Chang, Erwin, Carrier, & Cheever, 2010, p. 422) had higher verbal reasoning scores and were able to translate textisms to Standard English with fewer errors. This is further evidence of Graham and Hebert's work, *Writing to Read* (2010).

These writing gurus tell us that writing increases reading comprehension by furthering a learner's ability to analyze text, make connections, manipulate key ideas, and boost communication. For instance, writing a summary over a passage does more for comprehension than taking notes or using graphic organizers. Answering questions on a passage does even less to aid comprehension than note taking.

Even though directly teaching writing processes and structures greatly affects reading abilities, elementary teachers typically spend twenty minutes (or less) a day on writing. The majority of secondary content teachers—like science and social studies teachers—feel ill-equipped to teach writing. Many admittedly reduce assigning writing tasks and may assign only a one-paragraph assignment each month. This is far below the best practice recommendation of at least forty minutes a day of writing (and sixty minutes of daily reading) (Conley, 2005).

Misspellings such as "are" instead of "our" correlated with lower reading word scores. Recently, researchers analyzed relationships between the content of adults' and children's text messages and their achievement on standardized writing tests. They found no relationship between the children's grammar scores and common grammar texting violations but found a significant negative association between adults' achievement on the test and common grammar texting violations.

This study was one of the few naturalistic longitudinal studies that considered the specific types of text messaging errors used and categorized them. Researchers collected text messaging data at two points in time, one year apart. The tendency to make the same types of grammatical mistakes was unstable over the year because many times a word may be spelled differently within the same text message. Researchers say this illustrates the reasons behind using textism and human behavior more than signifies one's grammatical and spelling abilities or IQ (Wood, Kemp, & Waldron, 2014).

Overall, the results typically indicate texting as a positive influence on literacy for ten- to twelve-year-olds. In *Txting: The gr8 db8*, Crystal (2008) states:

> I do not see how texting could be a significant factor when discussing children who have real problems with literacy. If you have difficulty with reading and writing, you are hardly going to be predisposed to use a technology that de-

mands sophisticated abilities in reading and writing. And if you do start to text, I would expect the additional experience of writing to be a help, rather than a hindrance. (p. 157)

SPELLING

In the world of education, there has been an ongoing debate about the need for spelling instruction. With the invention of autocorrect and spell check, some believe valuable classroom time is wasted on teaching spelling. If it is to be taught, should it be embedded in the language arts curriculum or taught in a separate and isolated lesson? Should teaching spelling in isolation cease to be taught in secondary grades? Is a weekly list that's tested on Fridays the best way to teach kids to be master spellers? Surely, texting plays a role in how a student spells, right?

Even in a world of autocorrect and spell check, good spelling practices are foundational to great writing. Although spell check can be a helpful tool to those students who will take time to utilize it, it corrects only 30 to 80 percent of spelling mistakes within a composition (Montgomery, Karlan, & Coutinho, 2001). That is a large range, but it is based on how many homophones are used within the writing piece. For instance, a typical spell check program would not correct the homophone errors in the following statement: "To miles is two far too go."

With the heightened use of textese spelling, teachers have wondered whether it was in the best interest of the students to return to a traditional spelling curriculum: new list of twenty words on Monday and test on Friday. Educators always come back to the same conclusion. The traditional spelling methodology of teaching spelling in isolation is not effective in improving students' spelling. Students "memorize words in order to pass a test and don't make personal connections to the words, don't retain those spellings for future use, and in turn, don't make them part of their own personal vocabulary" (Suffern, 2008, p. 8).

Research has shown that learning to spell and read rely on much of the same underlying knowledge, such as the relationships between letters and sounds, and good spelling instruction can result in better reading (Ehri, 2000). Snow et al. (2005, p. 86) summarize the real importance of spelling for reading as follows: "Spelling and reading build and rely on the same mental representation of a word. Knowing the spelling of a word makes the representation of it sturdy and accessible for fluent reading."

Research also demonstrates a strong connection between spelling and writing. Struggling writers may spend valuable cognitive efforts (Singer & Bashir, 2004) trying to juggle handwriting, spelling, grammar, and punctuation—all elements that are automatic to strong writers. Instead, writers should be focusing on content, creativity, word choice, and audience. Poor spellers may restrict what they write to words they can spell, with inevitable loss of verbal power, or they may lose track of their thoughts when they get stuck trying to spell a word.

Mehta, Foorman, Branum-Martin, and Taylor (2005) found that, even if a student's comprehension grows during first through fourth grades, spelling scores drop dramatically by third grade and continue to decline. Progress in reading doesn't necessarily result in progress in spelling.

The average reader uses 10,000 words freely and can typically recognize another 30,000 to 40,000 words. To be an effective speller, one does not have to be able to correctly spell all the words in one's listening, reading, and speaking vocabulary. A vocabulary of 2,800 to 3,000 basic and well-selected words should form the core for spelling instruction (Fitzgerald, 1951; Horn, 1926; Horn & Otto, 1954; Monson, 1975; Rinsland, 1945). When choosing the words to include in spelling instruction, it's best to focus on high-frequency words (typically taught as sight words), regular spelling patterns, and frequently misspelled words.

It is best to teach regular spelling patterns because 50 percent of the words children read and spell have regular spelling patterns. These should be taught phonetically. Researchers found that the most successful approaches were based on structured spelling instruction that explicitly teaches speech sounds that are represented by the letters in printed words (Berninger et al., 2000; Graham, 1999; Swanson et al., 1999). The student identifies the individual sounds in a word and then chooses the correct letter (or letters) to represent each sound. Sometimes, the sound is represented by more than one letter (e.g., sh).

Students learn best from direct, systematic instruction that moves them along a continuum from the easiest sound/spelling patterns to the most difficult, such as consonants and short vowel sounds, consonant blends and digraphs, long vowel/final e, long vowel digraphs, other vowel patterns, syllable patterns, and affixes.

> "Eight words account for 18% of all the words students use in their writing, 25 words account for 33%, 100 words for 50%, 300 words for 65%, 1,000 words for 86%, 2,000 words for 95%, and 3,000 words for 97%" (Fry, Fountoukidis, & Kress, 2000; Horn, 1926; Otto & McMenemy; 1966, Rinsland, 1945). It's critical to prioritize these words in spelling instruction.
>
> However, if students master about 3,000 words, they have about 97% of the words they will need. (Allred, 1977, p. 222)

As teachers, we must provide a context for why students need the information we are trying to teach them. Some call this the framework for learning. When it comes to spelling, it may help adolescent spellers to understand they will be judged on their spelling regardless of the audience for which they are writing. Why give people the opportunity to judge them negatively as a writer? We can also frame the need for spelling practice by explaining that spelling is similar to athletic ability. Some people are naturally better spellers than others, and everyone can set a goal to improve their spelling.

Teachers would be wise to approach spelling with sensitivity and not become a spelling dictator. "Circling kids' misspellings, correcting them, taking off points for them—none of this has any benefit, and can sap kids' own motivation for spelling correctly" (Wilde, 2008, p. 11).

Instead, teachers should maintain a respectable tone toward the students and give them tips on how to become better spellers. This strategy is reflective of Dweck's growth mind-set, which speaks to the fact that everyone can improve, regardless of their current ability.

Middle school language arts teachers can point the students back to *why* spelling is difficult for them, which may come down to two factors: natural ability and the amount a student has read (Wilde, 2008, p. 14). Students can understand that spelling ability is much like athletic ability: Some people are more naturally inclined than others, and the more one practices the greater the skill becomes. The best training for a runner is to run. The best training for a reader is to read.

Middle schoolers who do not read will begin to have more crucial problems than just difficulty spelling. They should be encouraged to begin reading immediately and for a variety of purposes. Simply, exposure to words increases spelling power.

Carla Suffern, a middle school teacher from San Antonio, Texas, published "Teaching Spelling and Vocabulary with Greek Prefixes" (2008). Suffern confronts spelling when studying Greek and Roman mythology. She introduces the twenty of the most commonly used Greek prefixes and asks students to work collaboratively to recall words containing those prefixes in particular. Students then peruse the dictionary to add words containing the prefixes to their individualized and personal vocabulary/spelling list. They work with the words by creating images that are representative of meanings, and finally, they use the words in context while journaling. The spelling lessons are then embedded in the writing curriculum instead of being taught in isolation.

For students to master a word, they must manipulate it at least twenty-four times. Although it is improbable to expect students to write each spelling word twenty-four times, it's reasonable to consider consistent use in writing by providing a word wall (even for secondary students) or a personalized, self-created classroom dictionary.

Learning centers are another avenue for providing consistent exposure and practice to new vocabulary and spelling. In Dr. Katie McKnight's *Learning and Literacy Centers for the Big Kids*, she provides a plethora of ideas for teachers to expand their students' vocabulary and improve their spelling to more accurately express themselves in discussion and writing.

Spelling is not an issue limited to adolescents. Even if an adult sees a word misspelled, even one time, it can make it difficult to recall the correct spelling. Therefore, being consistently exposed to common textism misspellings can make it especially challenging to recall standard spellings. This is particularly difficult when the correctly spelled word has a concise and phonological abbreviation (Drouin, 2011), such as "thru."

Adults are considered to have a stable understanding of Standard English from consistent long-term use. If textese is creating challenges for adults to use correct Standard English, one can assume adolescents, who do not have a firm foundation of Standard English, are finding it even more problematic to recall correct usage and spelling.

EFFECTS ON MULTILINGUAL STUDENTS

Writing is a major obstacle for second language learners (Shafie, Azida, & Osman, 2010). Learners can acquire their first language naturally but still need formal writing instruction, and just because an individual can verbally communicate in a second language doesn't mean that he can communicate in writing to that same degree. Writing requires speaking, listening, and reading; therefore, it is the most challenging task for a language learner.

Various studies have concentrated on the differences in texting behaviors and literacy between foreign countries. One such study focuses on the texting influences of college students who use English as a second language. Participating professors and students believe that using textspeak harms the writing skills of English language learners.

Undergraduate students in Ghana displayed weak writing skills prior to entering the university. Professors encouraged students to be aware of differences between formal and informal writing; however, they found that when the English language skills are fragile, the use of texting may be detrimental (Dansieh, 2011). Therefore, professors encouraged students to avoid textisms until they've gained more control over the language.

In a study of Malaysian college students, it was found that using a high frequency of textisms made it difficult for the participants to recall correct spellings. Results further suggest that great use of textspeak shapes the language of only users who have weak English proficiency and students feel challenged when writing English because they often make spelling mistakes because of their texting habits.

A common challenge for English learners is to identify and comprehend idiomatic expressions. The English language is full of phrases like "don't beat around the bush," "it costs an arm and a leg," and "Elvis has left the building." Idioms are based on cultural references, and someone outside of the culture who can read takes these phrases literally and will need help making sense of them. Provide students with opportunities to expand their knowledge of language by examining idioms through cultural connections. Why don't we "put all of our eggs in one basket?" What does that mean and why do we say that? See chapter 5 for more ideas on teaching idiomatic expressions.

EFFECTS ON DYSLEXIA

Approximately 5 to 10 percent of children have language difficulties and impairments. By secondary school, that number reaches nearly 15 percent. Dyslexia affects children globally in varying degrees (Simoes-Perlant et al., 2012). It is characterized by "difficulties in learning to read despite conventional education, adequate intelligence, and sociocultural opportunity" (Simoes-Perlant et al., 2012, p. 67).

Children with dyslexia typically lag behind their peers in the areas of reading, spelling, phonological awareness, visual-attention processing disorders, and writing by two or more years. Symptoms of dyslexia include confusion between letters and words, reversal of letters and syllables or omissions and additions, problems with articulation of words, difficulty in segmenting syllables, and nonfluid and laborious reading. Similarly, dysorthographia, meaning difficulty in writing, displays symptoms in poor spelling, grammar, slowness, reversal of letters or syllables or omissions and additions (Moss & Dakin, 2008).

Researchers examined the texting habits of adolescent students with dyslexia. Although 100 percent of students possessed their own phone, only 42 percent used it for texting. They preferred to make voice calls. This is considerably less than the 92 percent nondyslexic students who reported using their cell phones for texting. When tweens with dyslexia and dsyorthographia send a text message, they use 10 percent less textspeak than nondyslexic writers (Simoes-Perlant et al., 2012). Writing is more laborious for adolescents with dyslexia or dysorthographia; therefore, the efficiency of texting doesn't necessarily apply (Simoes-Perlant et al., 2012).

Texting has been studied as a tool to assist individuals with language impairments. Researchers Beeson, Higginson, and Rising (2013) followed a man with aphasia, a speech impairment that also affects motor control, making it difficult for him to write by hand. After engaging in the researchers' procedure, this individual was able to better communicate through texting instead of using paper and pencil.

However, researchers also found that in terms of long-term memory, the patient benefited more from spelling words by writing by hand than practicing spelling the word through text. All in all, one will find fewer textisms in the writings of a student with dyslexia and less texting in general. Yet the same students willingly engage when they are able to interact with language in a playful manner without fear of failure (Veater, Plester, & Wood, 2011).

Typically, children with dyslexia lack confidence as readers. They will withdraw from literacy activities and do anything to avoid reading. Language impairments of any kind, whether dyslexia or even autism, can also create social isolation. Although they may avoid texting or writing-based activities, technology can provide a platform for communication that otherwise wouldn't exist.

Now, students have the option of voice-to-text technology. This tool alone has made an enormous effect for so many students on the spectrum of autism, not to mention those students who struggle with reading and writing. Witnessing a child who has never before communicated now being able to express himself and make connections with those around him is life changing. *Dylan's Voice* is a video produced by Apple about an adolescent boy who can now communicate using iPad technology. It's an excellent example of the miraculous role technology can play in the life of a struggling child.

Even those students who do not suffer from significant verbal language barriers but struggle with written communication can take advantage of iPad or voice-to-text technology. A typical homework assignment that can take hours because of the slow physical pace of writing can now be reduced to a manageable time frame. The student won't become physically and mentally exhausted, and it lessens the stress of evening homework for the entire household.

SOCIAL SKILLS

If you look around a restaurant or waiting room lobby, you will find more people on a device than those who are not; actually, you'll find about 80 percent on a device (Drago, 2015). They're texting, watching Netflix, or playing Candy Crush. Regardless of the task, eyes are glued to screens. If kids are lucky enough to have a device of their own, they become part of that 80 percent. If not, chances are they'll be squirming in their seats trying to gain the attention of the otherwise engaged parent. Over 90 percent of people (Drago, 2015) admit that texting is negatively affecting face-to-face (F2F) communication.

The greatest complaint comes from kids (Turkle, 2012). Kids, even teenagers, have been very candid about their feelings of neglect by parents who are constantly on a device. Sometimes, children even confess that they're on a device only because they're modeling their parents' behavior.

There's a body of research that tells us the overuse of devices negatively affects the development of social skills (Brignall & Van Valey, 2005; Drago, 2015; Misra, Cheng, Genevie, & Yuan, 2014; Turkle, 2012). The evidence is all around us in the lack of eye contact or in the preference of distant peers over present ones. Although social media platforms have been great for communicating with distant loved ones, they have damaged the relationships of those closest to us. When a device is present during a conversation, less empathy is given. Conversations will tend to be trivial and meaningless (Misra et al., 2014).

This brings us back to the discussion of language. Where do we acquire our most-used vocabulary? How do we learn the subtleties of human interaction and nonverbal communication? We learn it from our parents or caregivers, who are now prioritizing screens over conversations. The 7.5 hours of daily screen time *is* making a difference in our kids socially. However, we can't just point our fingers at the students. We as parents and adults in a community model the behavior our children reflect.

KEY POINTS

- College undergraduate students will use textspeak in social formats but will refrain from using texting language in professional or academic settings. The use of textisms is a conscious effort, primarily consisting of missing capitalization and punctuation, not incorrect spelling.
- Children can link an increase in their reading ability to when they began texting. The ability to use abbreviations and symbols for words requires the knowledge of linguistic rules. An individual must have a solid understanding of language to create and use an unconventional form of it.
- Writing a summary over a passage does more for comprehension than taking notes or using graphic organizers. Answering questions on a passage does even less to aid comprehension than note taking.
- Spelling ability is much like athletic ability: Some people are more naturally inclined than others. Reading is the best practice, and simple exposure to words will increase spelling power.
- Writing requires speaking, listening, and reading; therefore, it is the most challenging task for a language learner, and when the English language skills are fragile, the use of texting may be detrimental when trying to utilize formal Standard English.
- The 7.5-hour average of daily screen time is negatively affecting the development of social skills.

Chapter Three

Changing Perspectives

Society has always looked for a scapegoat. In the 1950s teachers accused poor academic work on bubble gum and the Beatles (McGraw Hill, 1952). Today, cell phones and video games are the explanation for underperforming, undisciplined, and distracted learners. Society tries to pinpoint the decline in education and achievement. Rather than viewing textspeak as a decline, we can view it as part of an evolution—of society, education, and language.

The way that technology is perceived influences the acceptance of textspeak into the classroom, whether as an uninvited guest or as a welcomed addition. Language is an invention that continually evolves. As Deutscher (2005, p. 47) states, "This invention is not the design of any one architect, nor does it follow the dictates of any master plan. It is the result of thousands of craving minds across the ages. So while language may never have been invented, it was nonetheless shaped by the generations."

Classrooms across the United States are leading students through scripted literacy programs, which lack individualism and stifle creativity. Canned writing approaches do not stimulate budding writers, create a love for the English language, or reflect the world outside of the classroom. The only way to provide a responsible education to modern students is if classroom practices are reflective of student life and real-world situations.

Linguists believe that language is interaction. The beauty of language can be watered down by constantly correcting its usage. Think of primary students. They love singing nursery rhymes, reading Dr. Seuss, and reciting tongue twisters. By the time they get to high school, only a fraction of students enjoy poetry. Why? Because we have sucked the fun out of language. Instead of allowing students to enjoy and attempt poetic devices, we've placed the emphasis on counting stanzas and analyzing rhyme scheme, which does not develop an appreciation of the literary work. When the focus is on interacting with the text, hearing it, reading it, and responding to it, a respect of language forms. Students are *interacting* with language instead of just analyzing it.

We know how critical it is for children to develop a love of reading early in life. From infancy, parents are encouraged to read to their child. The American Academy of Pediatrics promotes a large body of research on the connection between reading and brain development. The more parents read to their children at home, the more specific brain areas are activated, primarily areas supporting semantic processing. These areas are essential for language development as well as reading ability. Reading aloud, even in infancy, is directly connected to a child's ability to understand and acquire language. This concept extends to older children and adolescents. The more students are exposed to reading aloud, and the pleasure of reading, the greater the connection to understanding and acquiring language.

Once students reach secondary grades, the love of reading and language may be gone. Texting, or the utilization of textspeak in the classroom, may be just the hook you need to regain their interest. Inviting students to play with language through a variety of classroom activities and processes can help to rebuild that dissipated joy of reading or perhaps lay a foundation for those who haven't yet enjoyed it. Code-switching, when used correctly in the classroom, can be the catalyst for students to take something they already know and love, textspeak, and begin to build a foundation and appreciation for Standard English.

NEGOTIATING THE CODE

Code-switching is the skill of transitioning back and forth between formal and casual registers of language, depending on context and setting. In an academic setting that relies on technology, lines between codes can become blurred. This is especially true as more schools are moving to one to one, meaning each student is equipped with his own laptop or electronic device. Teachers will have to give explicit instructions about the type of language that is appropriate to use in each classroom platform, like discussion board forums or online communications between classmates. The majority of their academic work is now being housed in the same platform used for their entertainment and social exchanges. This can create blurred lines for adolescent brains.

Negotiating the code, or allowing students to help decide what rules of language will be followed during certain class activities, can assist both students and teachers. Teachers are encouraged to adopt a new flexible attitude toward language. Students receive direct instruction about writing contexts and gain ownership of their learning. Permitting students to journal or brainstorm in textspeak can aid their thinking and ultimately support their writing if it's the code that comes most naturally to them (Varnhagen et al., 2009). Teachers can develop and even model their personal journey toward digital literacy by reading and responding to educational blogs, increasing their social media networks, and contributing to educational forums.

Teachers are considered digital immigrants, and students are known as digital natives. Teachers often impose formal language on students and do not acknowledge the skill of code-switching as a valuable part of writing curriculum. The dismissal of this skill causes students to disengage from the writing experience because they view their instructors as dated or unenlightened.

It has taken nearly three decades to arrive at the process approach to writing that we presently have. Technology is advancing at breakneck speed, and we can't afford to wait decades for teachers to get on board with digital literacy practices. It is something that is happening now. If we do not participate, our students will be the ones left behind in an advancing world (Hawley Turner & Hicks, 2011).

As educators, we have a responsibility to teach our students to succeed in a rapidly changing digital world. Students must become digital writers and citizens so that they can contribute to the larger society of which they are part. "In the spirit of social justice, we believe that digital literacy is an emerging human right and that it is vital for community development and citizenship" (Hicks & Hawley Turner, 2013). We can't allow our discomfort with and trepidation of technology to hinder our students from becoming agents of social change.

As technology continuously changes, communication styles will most likely change too. Teachers are encouraged to adopt a new perspective of language: language as interaction and language as a process of trial and error. View all speakers as language learners because each of us continues to learn new vocabulary, develop various dialects, and learn new rules, depending on our changing social setting.

Youth interests and skills are highly mutable and fueled by rapid technological change. Even teachers who are under thirty cannot use their background as a template for the digital experiences of contemporary youth because many of the online social networks (like Facebook and Twitter) and other digital spaces youth currently inhabit (Instagram, Snapchat, and Musicly) barely existed a decade ago (Mahiri, 2012). Let's strive to have a better understanding of the actual experiences, interests, and skills of the young people in our classrooms so that we can create effective instructional designs.

DEVICE ≠ LEARNING

Even teachers who regularly utilize devices for educational purposes may not be doing it effectively. Teachers who pride themselves on the use of classroom technology may not be aware that they may actually be *limiting* student growth. For example, it is a common practice for teachers to set a guideline for the number of slides or links required in a PowerPoint presentation.

In reality, this type of parameter can confine student creativity just as the five-paragraph model may limit students' free expression and written voice (Hicks & Hawley Turner, 2013). A better practice is to model exemplary work and highlight that each example uses a different number of slides, illustrations, and links. A strong work is one that creates a complete statement, story, or idea and is not based on whether the work has ten slides and five links.

Online game–style quizzes and interactive graphs may engage a student but not necessarily challenge her thinking or further her understanding. Games with a team aspect do not guarantee students will learn to collaborate effectively in a diverse group of peers. Teachers must know how to utilize these tools effectively to produce a meaningful learning experience for students. If students are playing a feverish game of Kahoot!, then best practice is for each individual student to play on a personal device so that everyone is equally engaged.

Using a team device does not ensure engagement for all students. If teams are being utilized, then more meaningful discussion questions should be posed, questions that cause each student to have an individual role and be held accountable.

Another common mistake is the incorrect use of blogs. Blogging has become a popular resource for sharing information and connecting with others. The common format of a blog is "initiate-response-evaluate" (Hicks & Hawley Turner, 2013, p. 60). This invites others to collaborate, connect, and converse about topics of interest to all participants.

Often, teachers will invite students to create a blog as a means of demonstrating knowledge of content or as a formative assessment. Yet the term *blog* is in its true form used as a verb and not a noun. *Blogging* is writing, publishing, and inviting comment (Connective Writing, n.d.). This true form of blogging is rarely found in the classroom. Even when students are creating blogs or using devices, if there is a lack of critical thinking and problem solving at the center of the technology use, it will be no different than assigning a "keep busy" worksheet.

TECHNOLOGY VERSUS PEDAGOGY

Ruben Puentedura (2006), creator of the SAMR (substitution, augmentation, modifcation, and redefinition) model, outlines the use of technology in today's classroom. Similar to Bloom's Taxonomy, there are stages that progress in the quality of critical thinking. Bloom's foundational layer is memorizing facts and defining concepts. The level of critical thinking rises with each new level until the ultimate demonstration of learning has been reached, which is constructing an original work or idea. (See figure 3.1.)

The SAMR model also begins with lower-level critical thinking and moves to higher independent learning. The three bottom rows of Bloom's Taxonomy correlate with the two bottom layers of SAMR—categorized as enhancement—and the three top rows of Bloom's Taxonomy correlate with the two top layers of SAMR—transformative. (See figure 3.2.)

The SAMR model is helpful for teachers who already understand and are familiar with Bloom's Taxonomy and the concept of constantly moving students up the pyramid of thinking. Simply because teachers are now using a device doesn't mean they stop thinking about pedagogy. How is the device being used? If you can do the same activity with a paper and pencil, you're missing the advantages of the miracle we have at our fingertips.

The SAMR model can assist teachers in understanding how technology can be utilized in the classroom along with helping them evaluate their current instructional practices. Let's look at some classroom examples as outlined by Puentedura:

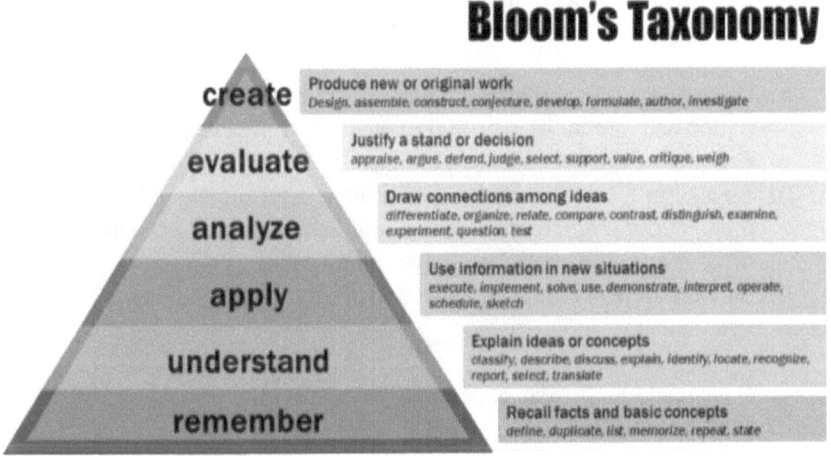

Figure 3.1. Bloom's Taxonomy

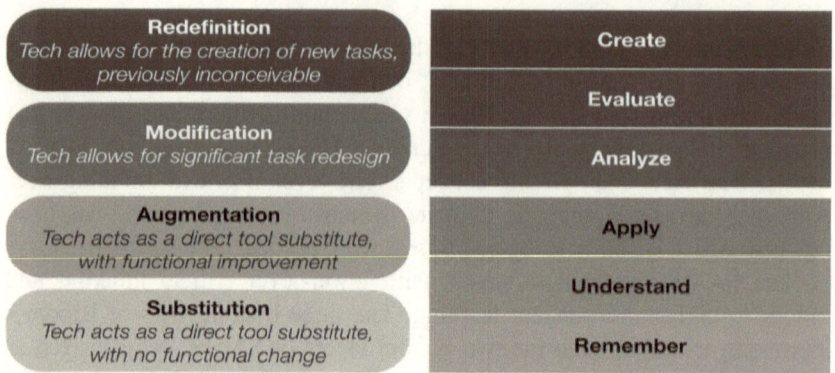

Figure 3.2.   SAMR and Bloom's Taxonomy: Assembling the Puzzle. Rueben Puentedura

- Substitution/Remember/Understand: Students use ebooks instead of trips to the library. Google Docs are used instead of college-rule notebooks.
- Augmentation/Apply: Google Docs are used for students to edit and collaborate with peers. Google Forms are used to assess student knowledge by automatically scoring and compiling data.
- Modification/Analyze/Evaluate: Develop a multimedia presentation.
- Redefinition/Create: Create an iMovie.

IMMIGRANTS TO CITIZENS

There are three strategies to transforming educators into digital literacy leaders (Hicks & Hawley Turner, 2013, p. 62):

1. Develop your own digital literacy. Begin by building a personal experience with digital literacy and interacting with education-based blogs, not only reading but also responding.
2. Engage in a larger conversation about digital literacy education. Another step is to increase social media networking. Contribute to open discussions on educational topics and reforms.
3. Support students in developing digital literacy. Model the process for your students.

Discuss the experience and encourage your students' journey to personal digital literacy growth.

NEW TEACHERS

When asked, preservice teachers shared that they experience a conflict between their personal view of writing and their philosophy of writing as a classroom teacher. The personal view tends to be more flexible and multimodal, whereas their professional perspective regards writing as traditional, with a focus on essential skills.

One research participant realized a stark contrast between his view of himself as a writer and his view of a classroom writing teacher: "They're really different to me. As a writer, I see all these liberal possibilities of what writing means, and yet when I get in front of my 6th graders it turns into a very formulaic and inflexible process" (Hawley Turner & Hicks, 2011, p. 63).

Both preservice and novice teachers are encouraged to further the evolution of literacy but often face obstacles, such as traditional school culture, pressures of standardized testing, and antiquated conceptions of writing. Many teachers in secondary English classrooms view digital writing as an addition to curriculum, not a part of their core instruction. With the focus on Common Core Standards for College and Career Readiness, teachers feel tasked with the instruction of each individual standard.

The integration of classroom technology becomes an additional list of skills to teach, not how the content is delivered and received. If curriculum is *what we teach* and instruction is *how we teach*, technology would then fall under the category of instruction. Typically, teachers view it as the *what* instead of the *how*. Yet the effective use of classroom tech makes it easier to deliver content to students, and the various platforms from which they can work to demonstrate understanding is more engaging.

In classrooms across the country, pressure is mounting on administrators and teachers to improve achievement data. This single-mindedness creates an extreme pressure to teach only what will be assessed. Many express fear of taking time to teach something that isn't necessary because it isn't on the state test (Hawley Turner & Hicks, 2011, p. 70).

Statistically, one-third of new teachers who work in high-needs areas leave the profession after only three years of service because of the aforementioned pressures and the inability to effect change in their schools and students (Kopkowski, 2008). Schools and communities must be willing to allow new teachers to influence their school culture in new and positive ways or risk losing potential catalysts of change.

Chapter 3

GRADING AND LANGUAGE

A body of writing has to be quantified, and this is not an easy task. The subjectivity in writing is well documented. One pertinent example is a research study of English teachers' grading practices. Starch and Elliot (as cited in Brimi, 2011) conducted a study titled "Reliability of the Grading of High-School Work in English." The authors sent two student papers to two hundred high school English teachers to be graded. The grades ranged from 64 to 98 percent on paper 1 and 50 to 97 percent on paper 2.

However, this study was conducted in 1912. Surely, within the past one hundred years, grading practices would have improved. At least that is what Brimi thought he would find when he replicated this study in 2011. Brimi had ninety freshman and sophomore English teachers, within a single district, receive eighteen hours of training on Northwest Regional Educational Laboratory's 6+1 Trait Writing Model of Instruction & Assessment, something Starch and Elliot didn't employ.

The 6+1 Trait Writing Model of Instruction & Assessment rubrics are well known across US classrooms because many state standardized assessments follow a similar format. The model evaluates Ideas, Organization, Voice, Word Choice, Sentence Fluency, Conventions, and +1, Presentation, when applicable. His findings were jaw dropping. The results were no better than his colleagues' results from one hundred years ago.

The well-trained teachers from the district who graded the same student paper ranged from 50 to 96 percent. There wasn't even a decrease in the range of scores. The challenge of grading is ubiquitous and touches every area of education. Even when there is a state-mandated grading scale, how each paper is scored will be graded differently by teachers within the same school and subject area.

Grade inflation may be the difference for high school students being college eligible and college ready. According to Conley (2008), nearly 40 percent of college freshmen need remediation courses. That number increases to 60 percent when we look at incoming students transferring from a community college. This is just one reason schools are moving toward standards-based grading (SBG) or a four-point rubric and away from a 100 percent grading scale. There are too many levels of subjectivity, and with a grading scale of 0 to 60 percent as an F, there are more levels of failing than there are of passing.

Why do we need so many levels to document a student's failure? Is a 30 percent score more reflective of failure than a 59 percent score? If grades are communication, either way we are communicating to that student that he didn't meet the expectation. The challenge in using SBG methods in secondary schools is translating a four-point rubric or standards-based grade into a GPA or a format interpretable by higher education.

We try to measure excellence in writing by correct spelling, word counts, and third-tier vocabulary. Writing can be difficult to quantify accurately with traditional grading practices. However, SBG practices close the gap of subjectivity and provide clearer feedback for students and parents. Review standards-based grading in Wormeli's revolutionizing book, *Fair Isn't Always Equal*.

RUBRICS

Holistic rubrics (see table 3.1) are quick and easy for educators to complete but provide no opportunity for students to grow their writing. Like any rubric, it should *be evaluating only the standard taught*, not timeliness, neatness, or behavioral expectations. Don't confuse a report of compliance with a report of learning (Wormeli, 2006).

Analytic rubrics (see table 3.2) are typically detailed and help students know where they stand in a variety of categories, but they are taxing for teachers to create and students rarely read the mass of details thoroughly. Another drawback to holistic and analytic rubrics is that they give a student a choice. Right away, a student can choose mediocrity by selecting a C (or 2-point paper, depending on whether you employ SBG) before ever beginning the writing process. If you choose to utilize a holistic or analytic rubric, consider listing only the highest descriptors.

Single-point rubrics (see table 3.3) are the simplest rubrics to create and provide the most helpful feedback to the student. Instead of front-loading the work by creating hefty rubric indicators, you are spending your time providing personalized feedback on each category, time well spent and preferred by students and parents. Single-point rubrics support the Love and Logic principles of *point and describe*. Identify the objective, identify where the student

Table 3.1. Clean Bedroom: Holistic Rubric

Score	Description
4	Bed is made using military corners, vacuum lines are clearly defined, floor is clear of all items, laundry is neatly folded and in correct drawers, room smells fresh, child is smiling.
3	Bed is well made, vacuum lines are apparent, floor is clear of all items, there is no evidence of dirty laundry.
2	Bed is sloppily made, the majority of toys and items are put away, hint of odor remains.
1	Bed has not been made, bedroom is disorganized, clothing items remain on floor, a mysterious odor lingers.

Table 3.2. Clean Bedroom: Analytic Rubric

	Beginning 1	Developing 2	Accomplished 3	Mastery 4	Score
Bed	Bed is not made	Bed is sloppily made	Bed is well made	Bed is made using military corners	
Floor	Floor is messy	Floor is clear of most items	Floor is clear, vacuum lines attempted	Floor is clear, clear evidence of vacuum lines	
Odor	Mystery odor evident	Hint of odor	No odor	Fresh odor	

is in relation to the goal, and identify what needs to happen to close the gap (Fay & Funk, 2010).

A teacher's typical response to this type of rubric is, "There is no way that I have time to give that much individual feedback for 185 students." Another common complaint is that students don't take the time to read the highlighted boxes in the analytic rubrics *or* read the personal comments teachers so carefully invest in making. Wormeli (2006) uses the analogy of grades as a GPS. Grades should tell you where you are, where you need to go, and exactly how to get there. This can't be done effectively through analytic-style rubrics.

Along with any other classroom procedure, students have to be taught how to utilize rubrics as part of the editing process. Here are some tips for getting students to use the feedback on rubrics to make changes to their writing:

- Teach reviewing rubrics the same way you teach close reading skills (*model, practice, model, practice, scaffold*).
- Provide class time for students to review comments and ask for clarification.
- Allow students to redo their assignment for full credit.

Rubrics can be overwhelming if teachers believe they have to develop rubrics for each alternative assignment. Whether students are presenting their knowledge via writing, sketching, or performing, the same rubric should be used. The rubric is a tool for documenting evidence of mastery of the *standard*, not evidence of mastery of the *platform*.

There is no perfect rubric. As you work on designing rubrics, remember its purpose (a GPS), define the evidence you will accept as mastery of the standard, and separate out any skills that are behavioral.

Table 3.3. Clean Bedroom: Single-Point Rubric

Concerns Areas that need work	Criteria Standards for performance	Advanced Evidence of exceeding standards
	Bed: Bed is made using military corners, is neat, and all bedding is clean.	
	Floor: Floor is clear of all toys and laundry, is vacuumed.	
	Smell: Room smells fresh and clean, no evidence of pets or shoes.	

KEY POINTS

- Negotiating the code, or allowing students to help decide what rules of language will be followed during certain class activities, can assist teachers in adopting a new flexible attitude toward language. Permitting students to journal or brainstorm in textspeak, because it's the code that comes most naturally to them (Varnhagen et al., 2009), can aid their thinking and ultimately support their writing.
- Even when there is a state-mandated grading scale, how each paper is scored has a great chance of being graded differently by teachers within the same school and subject area. Grade inflation may be the difference for high school students being college eligible and college ready.
- Even teachers who regularly utilize devices for educational purposes may not be doing it effectively.
- The SAMR model is helpful for teachers who already understand and are familiar with Bloom's Taxonomy and the concept of constantly moving students up the pyramid of thinking. Simply because teachers are now using a device doesn't mean we stop thinking about pedagogy.
- Digital language is an alternate language, which is appropriate when used in the right context. Code-switching refers to the ability to maneuver between academic writing and digital writing, based on which better fits the situation.
- There is no perfect rubric. As you work on designing rubrics, remember their purpose (a GPS), define the evidence you will accept as mastery of the standard, and separate out any skills that are behavioral.

Chapter Four

Flipping the Switch

Teachers are the keepers of the English language. There is no other role in society that governs language like that of a teacher. Who else controls and perpetuates spelling, usage, pronunciation, and rules? Reading is the decoding of signs and symbols to gain meaning, and there are an infinite number of ways to achieve this. Who says that the only acceptable signs and symbols are those of Standard English? Well, usually teachers say that.

Perhaps it is fear that keeps the guardians of language from accepting new codes or symbols, like changing the old English spelling of *through* to the phonetic spelling of *thru*. Conceivably, the more changes allowed, the less control remains in the hands of the guardians. Control is gained through insisting consistency in language. This ensures that the English language can be preserved and passed down.

The advent of textspeak poses a great threat to the guardians. This new language is permeating every area of society and bombarding students in every communication platform of their lives. It is impossible to stay ahead of the changes as new words and symbols created are added daily to vocabulary. Each year *Webster's Dictionary* adds more than one thousand words. The majority of those words are slang or new terms created by pop culture.

Chances are, the reason you gravitated toward this book is because you are dealing with textspeak in your classroom right now. You may have tried banning cell phones along with any form of casual register from your classroom. How is that working out?

TECH RELIANCE

Beyond informal writing styles and nontraditional spelling, Generation Text is known for prioritizing technology over courtesy. Go into any restaurant and watch couples scrolling through their newsfeeds instead of engaging in date-night conversation. Likewise, family outings are apparently railroaded by the device in each member's hand. It's become a third arm. When we are without our trusted device, studies show separation anxiety can occur.

Typically, separation anxiety develops in children under the age of twelve who have experienced a trauma, which may have caused them to be separated from an attachment figure or place of security. The definition of separation anxiety was extended to individuals of any age who experience excessive worry about being away from home or family members. The dependency on cell phones has become so acute that without them individuals may experience the same symptoms of anxiety and distress (Separation Anxiety, n.d.).

In fact, many studies are being conducted around the country (Rosen, 2015), all with the same results. Frequent cell phone use can cause anxiety, and that anxiety causes us to perform poorly academically and socially. This type of anxiety has been coined FOMO, or fear of missing out, and it's something that excessive cell phone checkers most likely have, which is the majority of people under thirty-five.

It's an addiction, and when we're separated from our drug, it can produce physical results: increased heart rate, heightened blood pressure, and even nausea. Studies indicate feeling pleasure when users check their cell phones after a period of nonuse. This feeling of pleasure is the release of the brain chemical dopamine and is the same response addicts receive from drug use. The release of dopamine helps humans connect pleasure and reward with necessary actions for survival, such as eating and sex.

Author Dr. Larry Rosen (2015) suggests pinpointing the feelings you associate when checking your phone. For example, identify why you check your phone.

- Did you receive an alert, or is it out of habit that you check every ten minutes?
- More importantly, what were you feeling when you checked your phone? Were there any symptoms that indicated FOMO?
- Which apps did you check? Were you looking to see whether you missed any information, such as new text messages or Facebook posts?
- Did you feel pleasure based on your search results? Or did you feel relief that you didn't miss anything?

Also, when you leave the house, where do you carry your phone? In your hand for quick-draw response or in the bottom of your bag or purse? If you leave it at home, will you turn around and go get it because you couldn't stand the thought of being an entire day without it or because it's necessary for completing the tasks you have that day? How long does it take you to answer a call? How long does it take you to respond to a text message?

Answering all of these questions may help make educators (and their students) become aware of how strong their cell phone dependence may be. If we can be aware of our need, then we can begin to adjust our actions accordingly.

Adolescents are the largest population of cell phone users. Heavy cell phone users carry it in hand or in a back pocket for quick retrieval and may even experience anxiety when separated from their trusty device. If separation causes decreased concentration and performance but having devices hinders social skills and common courtesy, then we may need to rethink our school policies in light of this information.

Approaching student technology use like the Prohibition isn't the best answer, although it is a common one. This type of policy only amplifies the problem of students being discourteous when using technology because they're not taught how to use devices appropriately (Frey & Fisher, 2008). A no cell phone policy can limit opportunities to teach students positive social skills. Replacing a no cell phone policy with a courtesy policy is a more effective strategy. If our goal as educators is to teach students to become educated and responsible citizens, then appropriate courtesy falls under that domain.

Educators could argue that teaching becomes impossible when cell phones are present because they create too much distraction, but the same arguments were made about one-to-one technology and the presence of iPads and laptops. Teachers everywhere have creative solutions when it comes to classroom policies. Pocket charts make great cell phone caddies for storage upon entrance into the classroom, but students can be given the privilege and responsibility of cell phone use during the day as long as it does not become discourteous to the teachers or peers.

Adoption of the courtesy policy helps students learn the necessary digital etiquette to promote positive face-to-face interaction and social skills and can lessen students' anxiety about their iPhone separation. Weaning adolescents from their devices will not be an issue easily corrected. It is a cultural issue, not only a classroom one. However, teaching students when to use smartphones appropriately to retrieve information as needed may be a good start.

THE BASICS

When it comes to writing assignments, whether your students are in third grade or senior AP English, begin by negotiating the code. Have a discussion with your class where you collectively decide what code, or register, is appropriate for the immediate task at hand. The basic language registers to teach can also be found in Ruby Payne's *Framework for Understanding Poverty* (2005):

- Frozen: unchanging (Lord's Prayer, wedding vows)
- Formal: academic language, specific vocabulary, appropriate word choice (giving a speech, writing a cover letter)
- Consultative: similar to formal but in conversation (how you might speak to an employer on a job interview or a teacher)
- Casual: hand gestures used in verbal exchanges, slang, incomplete sentences, colloquial (talking with friends, textspeech)
- Intimate: terms of endearment or intimate conversation (between lovers)

Teaching students the language registers and brainstorming with them various contexts when each would be used will help students to begin to identify and connect language and context. Payne also mentions that although it's not advised, it could be acceptable to move up or down one register. (When talking with a teacher, a student may get by with speaking in the casual register.) However, moving two registers is unacceptable and inappropriate. (When talking with a teacher, a student uses terms of endearment.)

Students relish opportunities to explore and share their cultural identities. Language is often the greatest evidence of an individual's geographic and ethnic culture. Allowing students to explore their identity through the language they use can be an experience in self-awareness and a connection back to a culture they love.

Ask students to identify which register is used when thinking. This will encourage students to reflect and identify their primary language. Primary language, usually defined by what language you speak every day or were taught by your parents, does not have to be limited to English, Spanish, or Arabic. Drill down to the actual dialect and register in which students communicate. That is the space where their primary language lies, that voice they hear when they think. Many students will write how they hear things, just as a Hoosier kid might spell "warsh" if that's the dialect used at home.

Allowing students to write, brainstorm, and journal in a language with which they are most comfortable, whether it's textspeak or Spanglish, creates a classroom environment of acceptance and cultural appreciation. If students are journaling or collaboratively brainstorming for a research project, then their primary mode of communication should be acceptable. For most students, this will most likely *not* be Standard English. Students may find it easier to get thoughts out if they do not have to translate to formal language during the process.

During a research writing process, students will read excerpts from articles and peer-reviewed journals. Examine the writing of these documents, and contrast the language used with your classes's previous work. How does it differ from higher academic writing? What does the writing style, vocabulary, word choice, and tone say about the author? Students quickly identify the expert tone of the formal writing style and the credibility easily given to works with specific and well-thought-out academic word choice. This can be done in every subject area and with any writing assignment.

Translating text calls upon a student's highest order of thinking. To translate, one must decode, read for meaning, synthesize the information, formulate ideas, and then reassemble the information in a new way while keeping in mind appropriate vocabulary and tone. This function is an excellent form of formative assessment to gauge the depth of student understanding. One way to engage students in this task is to ask them to pull up recent text messages or chat history. Ask them to rewrite the message as if they were writing it to the principal or an employer, all the while reviewing the discussion on language registers.

Sydney Redigan's freshman English class struggled through *Romeo and Juliet*. Her Detroit classroom consisted of over 90 percent English learners, and students struggled with the unfamiliar Elizabethan language. After the second act, she began having students "stop and write." Each stop and write consisted of a 140-character summary (the original text message length) and a translation exercise.

By keeping the summary to 140 characters, students have to be careful in their choice of facts and words. The translation was an excerpt of dialogue from a pivotal point from the scene. Students were instructed to take the Shakespearean dialogue and rewrite the Elizabethan script into a texting conversation. All were engaged in the activity, and for the first time all semester, she had 100 percent assignment completion.

Because this activity was successful, she also used a similar strategy when reading *To Kill a Mockingbird*. Students translated excerpts that contained a high density of Southern colloquialisms into modern textspeech. This helped the urban students who weren't familiar with Southern dialect to break down vernacular such as "breeches" and "yessum."

Third-year teacher Megan Milner was finding her seventh-graders struggling to comprehend grade-level text. Students could decode the text but were not able to retell or summarize the information. Megan took the approach of "breaking down text" with her students using a passage from *Robinson Crusoe*, which is far greater text complexity than her students' current level. She walked through the process with her class. Then, she asked the students to summarize the passage in five words or less. After reducing the text to its core essence, students were asked to further simplify it by translating it to textspeak.

The class essentially broke down a verbose and lengthy paragraph to three to five critical words. Summarizing is a skill with which secondary students still struggle, oftentimes, regurgitating details instead of getting the big picture. The process of breaking down texts helps students sift through details and uncover the meaning. Students comprehend the passage in a depth they wouldn't normally reach, including identifying the author's tone and inferences. Students gain immense pride in completing college-level analysis. One student exclaimed, "That makes so much more sense now." Another stated, "Well, why didn't he just say that?" It's a valuable lesson to the students to learn that what the authors are saying sometimes takes a little work to uncover.

The process of breaking down text is a most basic comprehension strategy. Once the students understand what the text is about, the code-switching comes much easier and extends their knowledge even further. For instance, when students are analyzing *A Christmas Carol*, the dialogue between characters can be translated into textspeak. This can be done on a Word document or using a website such as ifaketext.com, which creates screenshots of text messages you author. Students can also pair up to text one another their interpretations of one character's speech to another's.

One practice educators can be guilty of is focusing on the product of learning instead of the process of learning. We grade the final product of a student's work, and students assume this is the most valuable component of the learning process. If we study a unit for several weeks, we measure student learning through a unit test or a project presentation. It is the students' understanding that the learning process is just the buildup for the test or presentation. It is easy to see why kids perceive learning this way. The emphasis is on assessment and measuring growth. The focus is *the test* or the outcome.

However, this is not where learning takes places. The *process* is the space where the learning occurs. The old adage "It's about the journey, not the destination" is true with learning. During a close-reading activity, students are required to read a passage multiple times, each time focusing on a different aspect of the reading. They then summarize the passage and interpret the meaning in their own words. Once they've completed the close-reading activity, they submit it for grading. Their focus is on turning in that assignment for a grade, and although that may be necessary for accountability, it is the least important aspect of the process. Each time students read the passage, decode unfamiliar words, or translate new phrases, they are deepening their understanding. Therein lies the magic. Students and teachers both must be reconditioned to focus on the process instead of the outcome.

ADAPTING

Attitude is everything, and your attitude toward textspeak and technology in general is evident to your students and to your colleagues. Having a positive outlook on technology and an acceptance of the evolution of language will only aid your outlook on student writing. Begin by increasing your social media networking. Facebook, LinkedIn, and Google Groups are great places to start. Try responding to text messages from friends by using some of the more popular lingo—even if it makes you uncomfortable. (That may mean not using complete sentences or editing and revising a text message before you push send ;-)

Discover blogs that relate to your interests in the field of education to which you can subscribe. Then read and respond. Contribute to educational forums. Many state department of education websites host forums based on areas of specialization or licensing. Participate in the larger conversation on the effects of technology and changing language. Converse with your faculty and colleagues about what skills are needed to be successful in a digital world.

Consistently listed among the most important criteria for success are critical thinking, creative problem solving, and people skills. Spelling and grammar skills have yet to be mentioned as a priority in twenty-first-century education. Friends, let's keep perspective. Reading, writing, and the ability to communicate clearly are the foundations for success in higher education and a platform for greater contribution to society. (Yet there are still many highly successful men and women who struggled with reading and writing: Richard Branson, Steven Spielberg, and Charles Schwab, to name a few.)

In a world with voice-to-text and autocorrect, should our focus be spelling and grammar? When Albert Einstein, the scientific genius, was asked a basic question, he could not respond offhand. Instead, he explained that he did not carry such information in his mind that he could so easily get from a book. As teachers, why should we spend so much of our day teaching students things that can already be found in books or autocorrected?

KEY POINTS

- Frequent cell phone use can cause anxiety, and that anxiety causes us to perform poorly academically and socially. This type of anxiety has been coined FOMO, or fear of missing out, and it's something that excessive cell phone checkers most likely have, which is the majority of people under thirty-five.
- A no cell phone policy can limit opportunities to teach students positive social skills. Replacing a no cell phone policy with a courtesy policy is a more effective strategy. If our goal as educators is to teach students to become educated and responsible citizens, then appropriate courtesy falls under that domain.

- Teaching students the language registers and brainstorming with them various contexts when each would be used will help students to begin to identify and connect language and context.
- Allowing students to write, brainstorm, and journal in a language with which they are most comfortable, whether it's textspeak or Spanglish, creates a classroom environment of acceptance and cultural appreciation.
- Translating text calls upon a student's highest order of thinking. To translate, one must decode, read for meaning, synthesize the information, formulate ideas, and then reassemble the information in a new way while keeping in mind appropriate vocabulary and tone.

Chapter Five

Classroom Practice

As you implement code-switching activities in your classroom, consider beginning with translanguaging activities that explore various registers of communication and popular textisms. Also, consider sharing these activities with content-area teachers because multiple exposures to comprehension strategies will reiterate skills for students. The following pages include activities that are available for download on www.drjennyfrench.com.

ACTIVITY 1: IDENTIFYING FORMAL AND CASUAL WRITING

Start by reviewing the registers of language with students. Ruby Payne's five registers of language are available for reference, or simply have students identify formal, or academic, tones from casual speech. In the following activity, students can place an "F" for formal or a "C" for casual next to each sentence.

 **Formal vs. Casual Writing**

Identifying Formal and Casual Writing. In the following activity, students can place an "F" for formal or a "C" for casual next to each sentence.

1. What could possibly detain you from this event?
2. I found his attitude to be particularly negative.
3. Her classwork is quickly deteriorating.
4. I just don't get this and I've read it a million times.
5. Why didn't you show up last night?
6. I'd be great at this job because I learn fast and try hard.
7. She quit trying with school work and stuff.
8. I would be an excellent candidate for this position due to my countless efforts and my ability to learn quickly.
9. Regardless of how many times I read the material, I am unable to fully comprehend it.
10. Her lackluster efforts in academic studies are evident.

Figure 5.1.   Identifying Formal and Casual Writing

ACTIVITY 2: IDENTIFYING THE FIVE REGISTERS OF LANGUAGE

This activity reviews the language of each of the five registers of language based on Ruby Payne's work.

1. Mrs. Jones, may I speak with you after class?
2. "Our Father, who art in heaven, hallowed be thy name."
3. Your eyes are as blue as the ocean.
4. Can you hang after practice?
5. It's in our best interest to defer the decision until the results from the next survey are available.
6. I appreciate your time and look forward to talking with you more.
7. Why are you freaking out?
8. Students between the ages of 8 and 18 spend on average 7.5 hours a day interacting with media.

Figure 5.2. Identifying the Five Registers of Language

ACTIVITY 3: CODES AND CONTEXT DISCUSSION

If you ever visited Starbucks, you may have noticed that they have a very specific code. You will most likely hear someone order a *venti* water with ice instead of a large ice water, or someone may ask for a *tall* chai tea instead of a small. However, when you visit Dunkin Donuts, this vocabulary wouldn't be appropriate because that code isn't used there. There are many examples where a code of language is appropriate only in a specific context. Brainstorm other examples with your class. Close the discussion by asking why it's important to have one code (Standard English) that can be used by everyone.

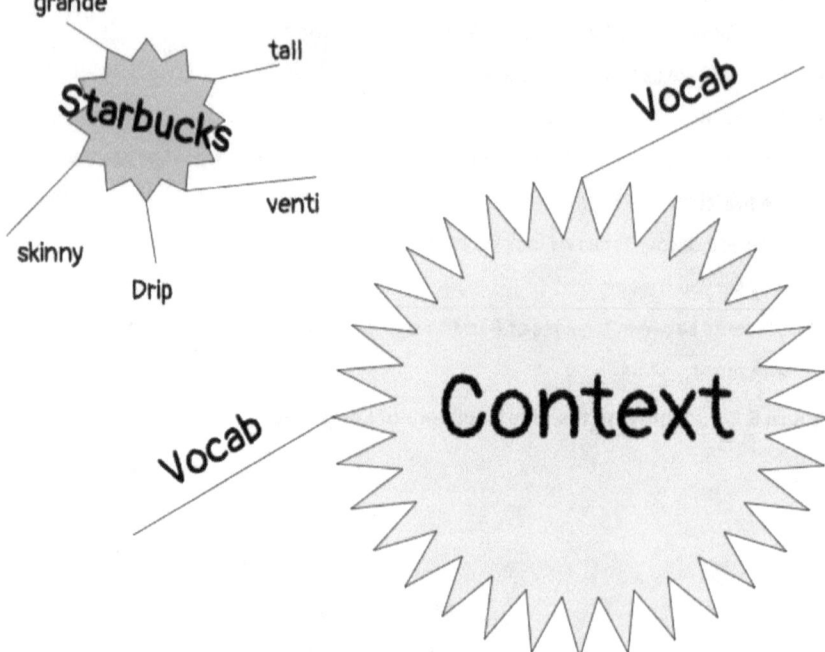

Figure 5.3. Codes and Context

ACTIVITY 4: CODE-SWITCHING ANNOUNCEMENT

Consider having students write an announcement for an upcoming school event. The announcement must be written for three audiences: peers, parents, and city officials. Ask students to write using language appropriate for each context. Also, ask students to decide the best mode of communication for each announcement. A sample follows.

Code-Switching Announcement

Audience: Peers	Audience: Parents	Audience: City officials
Platform: School announcements, fliers around building	**Platform:** School newsletter home & school website	**Platform:** Email to each official
Announcement: Come see your friends in Beauty and the Beast Next Sat & Sun @ 7! Students are free!	**Announcement:** Middle School Drama Department Presents: Beauty and the Beast Saturday & Sunday 7pm Tickets: $3	**Announcement:** Dear Sirs and Madams: The Taylor Middle School Drama Department will be presenting Beauty and the Beast on Saturday and Sunday, March 17th and 18th, 2018. It would be our greatest pleasure for you to attend. Sincerest regards, TMS Drama Department

Figure 5.4. Code-Switching Announcement

ACTIVITY 5: LANGUAGE REGISTERS IN LITERATURE

To further a classroom connection, read aloud an excerpt from the writing styles of Tom Sawyer and Shakespeare. Tom Sawyer's novels are written using a strong Southern dialect, which is a stark contrast to that of the Elizabethan English used in Shakespeare's writing. Discuss the difference in the language used and what can be inferred about the author and characters represented. Compare these to the tone of a scientific journal article, and ask the students the following questions.

LANGUAGE REGISTERS IN LITERATURE

After reading an excerpt from Shakespeare, Tom Sawyer, and a scientific journal, respond to the following questions.

1. How is the language different in each of these texts?
2. In what language register is each text written?
3. What does the language register tell us about the characters?
4. Based on the language register only, which character would you want as your teacher? your doctor? your friend? Why?
5. What does the language *we* use tell people about us?

ACTIVITY 6: TEXTSPEAK GLOSSARY

Once students are confident in differentiating casual and formal text, allow students to create their own textspeak glossary, or try reviewing the Textspeak Glossary at the back of this book. Students can identify alternative textisms or ones that are not included. Because language adaptations take place on a regular basis, it is safe to assume that the glossary is not all encompassing.

ACTIVITY 7: MATCHING TEXTISMS TO PROPER ENGLISH

Another foundational exercise is to have students match textisms with proper English expressions.

Table 5.1. Matching Textisms to Proper English

Textism	Proper English
1. r u	a. your
2. b4	b. kiss, kiss
3. l8r	c. are you
4. oic	d. too cute
5. lol	e. bye bye
6. ur	f. oh, I see
7. xx	g. later
8. cul8r	h. before
9. 2QT	i. laugh out loud
10. bibi	j. see you later

1.C 2.H 3.G 4.F 5.I 6.A 7.B 8.J 9.D 10.E

ACTIVITY 8: TRANSLATING TEXTSPEAK

In the following activity, students can translate the common text messages into full sentences in proper English. Then, students can create their own text messages and have a classmate translate them into proper English.

TRANSLATE TEXTSPEAK PHRASES

Write the following sentences properly:

1. CM ASAP:
2. CUL8R:
3. b w8ng 4u:
4. w@ u doin 2day:
5. ur 2QT:

Write five text messages for your partner to write properly:

1.
2.
3.
4.
5.

Answers:

1. Call me as soon as possible.
2. I will see you later.
3. I'll be waiting for you.
4. What are you doing today?
5. You are too cute!

ACTIVITY 9: TRANSL8IT

Transl8it.com is a website for translating texting language. This is a helpful resource for teachers to reference if they are unfamiliar with textisms, but it is even more popular with parents for decoding text messages sent by their children.

ACTIVITY 10: SUMMER VACATION ESSAY

A thirteen-year-old Scottish girl wrote an essay about her summer vacation. This particular essay become the focal point of much discussion in news media because the entire essay was written in textspeak. Below is an excerpt from her essay and a translating activity (British Council, 2012).

SUMMER VACATION ESSAY

The following is an essay written by a thirteen-year-old student. Read the essay, and translate it into proper English on the lines below.

My smmr hols wr CWOT. B4, we used 2 go 2 NY 2C my bro, his GF & thr 3 :- @ kds FTF. ILNY, its gr8. Bt my Ps wr so {:-/ BC o 9/11 tht thay dcdd 2 stay in SCO & spnd 2 wks up N. Up N, WUCIWUG -- 0. I ws vvv brd in MON. 0 bt baas & ^^

_____
_____
_____
_____

Answer:
My summer holidays were a complete waste of time. Before, we used to go to New York to see my brother, his girlfriend, and their three screaming kids face-to-face. I love New York; it's a great place. But my parents were so worried because of the terrorism attack on September 11 that they decided we would stay in Scotland and spend two weeks up north. Up north, what you see is what you get—nothing. I was extremely bored in the middle of nowhere. Nothing but sheep and mountains.

ACTIVITY 11: TEXTSPEAK NOTE TAKING

Once students have had a chance to review common textisms, allow students to take notes using their own version of textspeak or shorthand. Emojis and sketches would also be appropriate for this exercise. Try getting the science and social studies teachers on board for this activity. Discuss why this type of writing is appropriate in the context of note taking. Have students read the excerpt and discuss the following questions.

TEXTSPEAK AND NOTE TAKING

Although the textism phrases are now widely recognized, they are not new inventions. Think of the telegraph. This was a turning point historically for communication. The system was created in the 1840s by Samuel Morse, who developed the system for transmitting electrical signals using a code he developed by assigning dots and dashes to each letter of the alphabet. When communication is costly or cumbersome, abbreviations are necessary, and Morse Code is the prime historical example (MacKenzie-Hoy, 2006, para. 3).

Stenography, or shorthand, was also invented to expedite communication. Stenography uses the same approach to communication as texting: symbols and abbreviations. Furthermore, stenography is based on phonetic spelling! Shorthand dates back to ancient Greece but most widely became used around 63 BCE in the Roman Empire. Over thousands of years, versions of shorthand have come and gone and have been translated into almost every language. In 1837, an educator by the name of Sir Isaac Pitman developed the most widely used shorthand system based on omitting vowels; the same strategy is used in textspeak. Stenography continued to evolve, and in 1893 schools began teaching shorthand to students as a necessary business skill (Shorthand, n.d.). Later, shorthand was adapted as a system for typewriter use. Sixty rules are applied to abbreviate more than twenty thousand words. Comparably, there are 227 pages in the "online textlingo dictionary" listing the most commonly used textspeak abbreviations.

In 1906, a Stenograph machine was invented and used to aid court reporters. A Stenotype machine was also invented and used to record speech. "Both machines have keyboards of 22 keys. Because the operator uses all fingers and both thumbs, any number of keys can be struck simultaneously" (Shorthand, n.d., para. 5). Hmmm, that sounds familiar. Text messaging employs both elements used by these machines: typing with multiple fingers and thumbs and mimicking a voice-to-text feature.

In 1985, a member of the Global System for Mobile Communication (GSM) by the name of Friedhelm Hillebrand wanted to develop a text messaging system to use with the car phones. The limited bandwidth would allow for only short messages (Milian, 2009). After experimenting, he found that most messages could be effectively communicated in 160 characters per message, which was similar to the length of a standard postcard.

Various connections can be made between shorthand and texting. Nearly three hundred research studies have been done on the reading and writing of shorthand. The results indicate that "Good readers of shorthand were also good readers of print" (Anderson, 1981, para. 3) and habits that were formed early during the learning of shorthand persisted throughout the course of using it (Anderson, 1981). One study (Bloom, 2010) found that there was an increase in the reading ability of children when they began texting, illustrating that an individual must have a solid understanding of language to use an unconventional form of it.

Discussion Questions:

1. Textspeak is not a new idea. What does this tell us about society and communication throughout history?
2. Why is it necessary to abbreviate communication, then and now?
3. The article mentions that "good readers of shorthand were also good readers of print" and that "there was an increase in the reading ability of children when they began texting." Why do you think these statements are true?

Classroom Connection:

Have students try inventing and practicing their own version of shorthand. This can consist of textisms, sketches, and emojis. Debrief with your students: Was your method effective? Why or why not? What would have to be done for all students to use your version of note taking?

ACTIVITY 12: GIST

You are most likely familiar with the summarizing strategy known as Gist. In this exercise, students read a passage and then summarize it in exactly twenty words. It is helpful for students to record the who, what, when, where, why, and how *or* list the key words from the article as they read. In this version, students must summarize the passage in *ten textisms*.

GIST

Read the passage, and as you read, highlight the keywords. Identify the five Ws, and then summarize the passage using *only ten textisms*.

Title: _____
Who: _____
What: _____
When: _____
Where: _____
Why: _____

_____ _____ _____ _____ _____
_____ _____ _____ _____ _____

ACTIVITY 13: RAFT

The RAFT writing strategy calls for students to identify their "R," role as a writer; "A," audience to whom they are addressing; "F," format of the writing piece; and "T," topic about which they are writing. Similar to Activity 4: Code-Switching Announcement, the RAFT strategy can be tailored to a variety of audiences, thereby differentiating the appropriate writing style.

Table 5.2. RAFT

Role: Student	Audience: TV viewers
Format: Letter to local news station	Topic: Explanation of TV ratings

    I am a middle school student, and I recently experienced something that concerned me. I was visiting a friend's house, and his seven-year-old brother was watching a television show rated TV MA. I asked my friend if his parents let them watch TV MA shows, and he had no idea what I was talking about. I explained to him that TV shows have ratings like movies do. Those ratings are there for a reason. MA stands for "mature" and is made for people over seventeen years old. This made me think that maybe not everyone knows the TV ratings, what they are and what they mean, so I would like for your station to do a news story on this topic.
    I think it would be a great idea and many families could benefit from it. Even if some of the ratings are obvious, some are not, and giving this information on the news could help a lot of people. For example, TV 14 suggests that kids under fourteen years old should watch that show with a parent. It doesn't mean they can't watch it at all though. This is just one example of how TV ratings could be better explained. It would protect what kids see, and parents know how to protect their kids.
Thank you,
Corbin L.

ACTIVITY 14: DUELING TEXTERS

Dueling texters is an activity that supports argumentative writing in a texting debate format. Depending on your classroom cell phone policy, students may actually text a partner and send screenshots of their dialogue to the teacher. If this is not an option for your students, try using iFaketext.com. Students would have to work in pairs and take turns entering their arguments and rebuttals within the program.

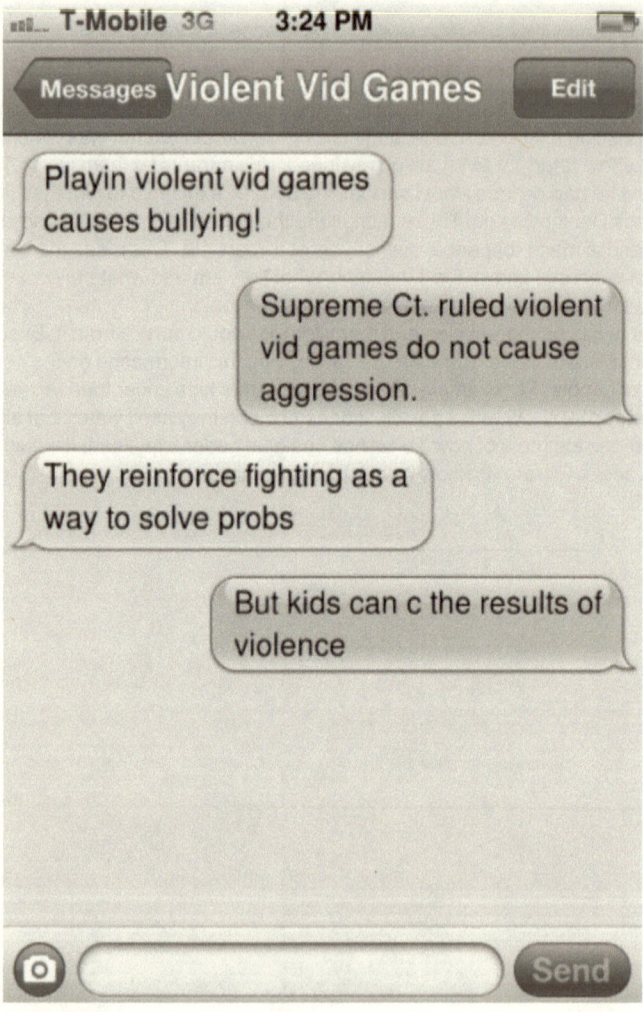

Figure 5.5. Dueling Texters

ACTIVITY 15: BREAKING DOWN TEXT

Breaking down text is a close reading–style strategy that guides students through the process of deconstructing the literature in order to reconstruct meaning. This is typically done with text that is significantly above grade-level text or a student's independent reading lexile. When teaching this strategy, it is critical to model the process and work through each step with your students until they can comfortably simulate the process independently. The first few paragraphs of *Robinson Crusoe*, by Daniel Defoe, is a great resource to use when modeling this strategy because it uses complex sentence structure and an eighteenth-century lexicon.

Begin by having students silently read a chunk of the text, like a page or a longer paragraph. After the initial cold read, have students change all punctuation to a period. When a text is longer or more difficult to read, it is common for a struggling reader to lose focus. By replacing a comma or semicolon with a period, it shortens complex phrases to more manageable chunks and allows the brain to remain focused.

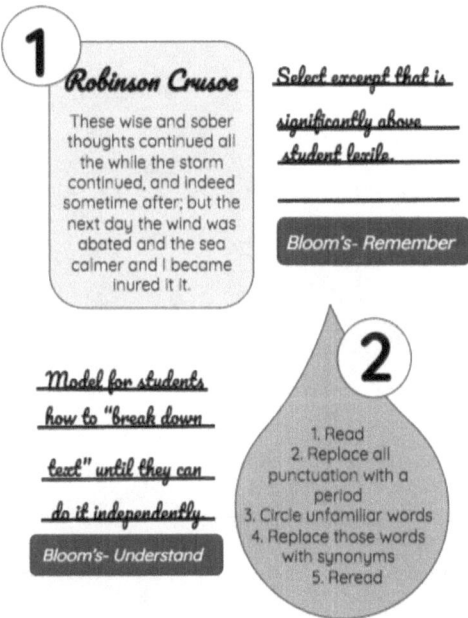

Figure 5.6. Breaking Down Text

Next, students will circle or highlight any vocabulary with which they're unfamiliar. Once this step is complete, students should have the opportunity to replace the identified words with more common synonyms. If the student isn't able to deduce the word by using context, allow the student to use a device to quickly look up the word using an online dictionary or thesaurus to replace the obscure word.

Once the text has been deconstructed through this process, meaning can be reconstructed. Ask students to reread the text utilizing the shorter sentence structure and new vocabulary. Depending on the level of ability, students should be able to complete a summary of what they've read reflective of their understanding.

Implementing the Gist strategy can also guide students through reconstructing meaning. Because Gist is typically used to summarize an entire article or passage, an alternative would be to have students create a five-sentence summary of the paragraph they've read. By limiting a summary to a five-word sentence, accuracy in word choice becomes crucial.

ACTIVITY 16: FLIP THE SCRIPT

Code-switching should be practiced by both switching formal to casual and casual to formal, especially when students grapple with complex texts like Shakespearean dialogue. The Elizabethan language is foreign to adolescent ears. Allow students an opportunity to explore the language by translating Elizabethan English to modern-day textspeak. This allows students an opportunity to break down the text and then reconstruct meaning through translating dialogue instead of summarizing.

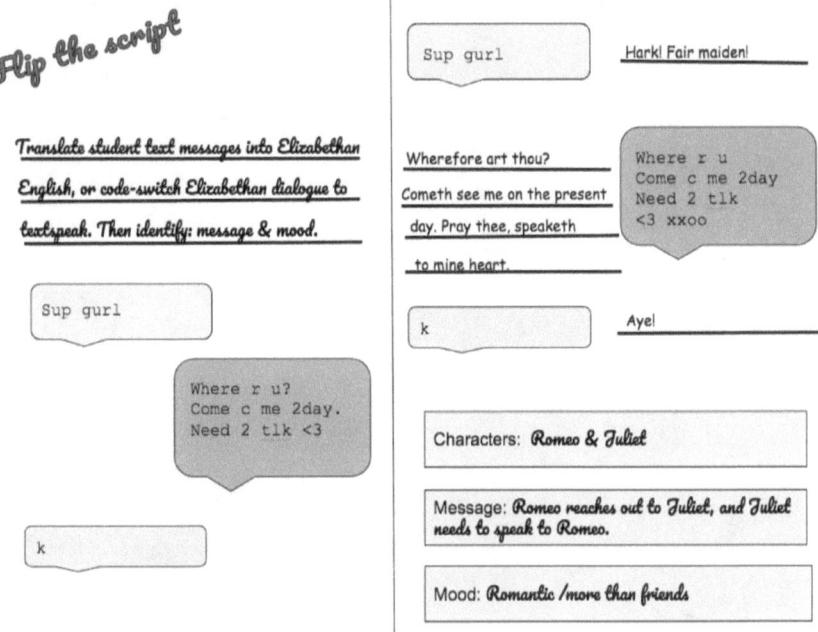

Figure 5.7. Flip the Script

ACTIVITY 17: IDIOMATIC EXPRESSIONS

Idiomatic expressions tend to be difficult for language learners. Never hand a long list of idioms to a new language learner. Idioms are best taught sparingly, verbally, and in context. If possible, introduce a few idioms a week, all centered around the same meaning, like the weather or wishing someone good luck. Have students create illustrations that represent the idiom literally and one that represents the true meaning. Students can present their work to the class, create posters, or share online. Most importantly, practice utilizing idioms in class on an increasing basis as students advance in fluency.

Research Study

As mentioned earlier, a few years ago I set out on my quest to prove that textspeech was ruining the English language. How did I do this, you might ask? The same way you go about proving any point . . . design a quantitative research study. Below you will find my Research Study, which is only one piece of the puzzle, but as with any study, I hope that it will further the understanding of language and learning.

DESIGN

A correlational study is used in this research project to determine whether there is any relationship between the independent variables, (a) frequency of sent texts and (b) student Free and Reduced Meal eligibility, and the dependent variable, writing achievement, which is measured using the writing portion of the state standardized test. There is no control group used in this study; rather the range of texts would create a scale by comparing individual students. A multiple regression analysis would be used to find the statistics of the data.

A multiple regression analysis investigates the relationship between more than one independent variable and one dependent variable. This test best suits this research design because the researcher is seeking to show a statistically significant difference in the mean scores between the two variable groups (Warner, 2013).

The effect size will be evaluated using Pearson r correlation. The effect size is low if the value of r varies around 0.1, medium if r varies around 0.3, and large if r varies more than 0.5 (Cohen, 1992). The data would then be displayed in a scattergram. This is a quasi-experimental study because class rosters and student schedules are preexisting and student participants cannot be randomly assigned.

The writing portion of the 2015–2016 ISTEP, Indiana's standardized test, was used to measure student writing achievement. The test scores that were used for this study were collected ex post facto. In other words, the test scores were administered and graded before the researcher began the study. Individual tests were pulled and examined, and the writing scores were recorded.

According to Crystal (2008), there is a likelihood of 94 percent of middle school students owning their own cell phones. This is true even of lower-income families. A federal program provides free Safe Link cell phones for every member of the family who qualifies for government health care or assistance (safelinkwireless.com). Therefore, socioeconomic status should not skew the results of the data because a wide range of students will be able to participate.

Time spent texting will not be considered because quantity is more likely an influencing variable. Although students may text during class, this would be a difficult factor to track and would be more likely to be included in a qualitative study.

RESEARCH QUESTIONS

RQ1: Is there a statistically significant relationship between frequency of texting and adolescent writing achievement?

RQ2: Is there a statistically significant difference in the effect of texting between adolescents eligible for Free and Reduced Meals and adolescents who are not eligible?

NULL HYPOTHESES

H01: There is no correlation between the frequency of text messages sent and the writing achievement of middle school students.

H02: There is no difference in the effect of texting on middle school students eligible for Free and Reduced Meals and students who are not eligible.

PARTICIPANTS AND SETTING

During the 2014–2015 school year, 506 sixth-grade students, 478 seventh-grade students, and 525 eighth-grade students attended this public middle school in central Indiana. In the population of 1,518 students, only 136 students pay full price for their meals. The remaining 1,382 students receive either free or reduced cost meals. These numbers indicate that 78 percent of the students of the middle school live below the state poverty guideline, which is $23,850 for a family of four in Indiana.

The middle school's student demographics are as follows: Caucasian 64 percent, Black 23 percent, and Hispanic 8 percent. Only 4 percent of the students are English language learners. Eighteen percent of the student population was regarded as special education students. Female students make up 44 percent of the student body, and males make up 56 percent of the student body.

The students performed as follows on the state standardized test, the Indiana Statewide Testing for Educational Progress (ISTEP): 52 percent of sixth-graders passed both Math and English Language Arts (ELA), 53 percent of seventh-graders passed both Math and ELA, and 51 percent of eighth-graders passed both Math and ELA portions.

The middle school is located in central Indiana. According to the United States Census Bureau, the town has a population of 55,554 (2012). Seventy-eight percent of the population is Caucasian and 15 percent are Black. Like many Hoosier towns, auto manufacturing served as a major source of revenue for the city and its residents in the 1940s and 1950s.

This town has a long history with the automotive industry, beginning in the late 1800s when natural gas was discovered. This discovery drew various manufacturing businesses to the area. In the 1970s, the city was home to approximately twenty General Motors manufacturing plants. Over time, these plants slowly began to close, and by 2005, none remained.

The school district serves a high rate of students in poverty. This is evident by the 78 percent of students holding Free and Reduced Meal status (2014) and a high school graduation rate of 57 percent (2010). Currently, the unemployment rate is 10 percent (2013), which is higher than the national average of 7 percent. The median income also dropped in Anderson in the past twenty years and now averages around $33,000 (United States Department of Labor Statistics).

The surveyed middle school is now the only public middle school in the city, and it has an approximate population of 1,500 students in grades six through eight. It has an area of forty-one square miles, which requires many students to ride a bus for forty-five minutes to one hour, each way. The school building was remodeled in 2012 after being transformed from a high school building into a consolidated middle school building. This remodel was done in hopes of improving the graduation rates.

Power analysis for a multiple regression with two predictors was conducted in G*Power to determine a sufficient sample size using an alpha of 0.05, a power of 0.80, and a medium effect size ($f^2 = 0.15$) (Faul, Erdfelder, Lang, & Buchner, 2007). Based on the aforementioned assumptions, the desired sample size is 68.

For this study, the number of participants sampled was 68 students, which according to de Winter (2013), "more is better" applies to statistical inference. According to the law of large numbers, "a larger sample size implies that confidence intervals are narrower and that more reliable conclusions can be reached" (p. 1).

Purposive sampling is used to locate a specific subset of people, which in this case is adolescents in grades six through eight attending the middle school who own a personal cellular device. This sampling method eliminates potential participants who do not fit the necessary profile or aid in the purpose of the study.

Parent consent forms and child assent forms will be made available to each student and parent on registration day. The students who have signed forms will be asked to complete the online survey. A question on the survey asks whether students own their own cellular device. If they answer no, the survey will end. If they answer yes, the survey will continue. This process will determine the number of students participating in the study.

INSTRUMENTATION

The main instrument used in this study is the Indiana Statewide Test for Educational Progress (ISTEP). The test was instituted because of the No Child Left Behind Act. The ISTEP has been used as a measurement for numerous research studies (Boone & Scantlebury, 2006; Davis, 2004; Missall, Mercer, Martinez, & Casebeer, 2012).

ISTEP was created by McGraw-Hill in 1987 and first administered in 1988. The test was given in the fall until the 2009–2010 school year and was then conducted in the spring. The motivation for changing the test season was to test students on the material of their current grade level in hopes that they would perform better.

When they were tested in the fall, students were performing lower because they were tested over academic standards they had learned the previous year and had to recall information they had learned up to a year prior to the test. At the present time, the writing portion of the test is administered separately in March, and the remaining test sections are given in late April (Indiana Department of Education).

The ISTEP is administered to all students in Indiana each year beginning in third grade through eighth grade and then again when students are high school sophomores. Students are tested in reading, writing, and mathematics. Students in fourth and sixth grades are also tested on science concepts, and fifth- and seventh-graders are tested on social studies content.

In this study, only the writing scores were collected and analyzed. The writing portion, called the Applied Skills Assessment, consists of short-answer and essay questions. The answers are scored according to a four-point rubric. The four categories scored are Ideas and Content, Style, Voice, and Organization. According to the official ISTEP writing rubric, "A Score Point 4 paper is rare. It fully accomplishes the task in a thorough and insightful manner and has a distinctive quality that sets it apart as an outstanding performance."

The second instrument used is a questionnaire completed by participating students. The questionnaire was validated by a university professor, a middle school data coach, a middle school math teacher, and two middle school Language Arts teachers. The questionnaire consists of eight questions. The first five questions gather data on the student: name, age, grade, gender, and name of Language Arts teacher last year (this is helpful when pulling student test scores).

Questions six and seven ask students about their personal cell phone history. Question eight requires students to calculate how many text messages they sent during a one-week period. Students will be provided with verbal directions and a worksheet to help them tally the number of texts sent. The worksheet is a simple form that helps students keep a tally of the number of texts to each contact and a place to add and record the total number of text messages. The questionnaire was put into a Google Form so that data could be easily recorded and compiled.

PROCEDURES

The initial step in the research process included creating and validating a questionnaire. Once it was validated, it was formatted into a Google Form survey. Parent consent forms were made available during student registration on July 30, 2016. There were sixty-four signed consent forms.

During the week of August 15, all building Language Arts teachers were emailed specific instructions on how to access the Google Form and complete the tally worksheet. The researcher organized all participants by homeroom teacher. Teachers were then emailed a list of the students in their homeroom classes who would participate in the study by completing the survey.

Participants were also asked to bring their cell phones to class during the time of the questionnaire. The middle school is a one-to-one school, and each student is provided a Google Chromebook for the academic year. This makes it easy and accessible for teachers to implement the survey. Question four asks students whether they have a personal cell phone. If they answer no, the survey will end, and their information will not be included in the study.

The last question on the survey asks students to use the tally worksheet to manually count all text messages they sent during the past seven days and enter the final number as the answer on the survey. As surveys are completed, data is organized and stored into a Google Spreadsheet. Once questionnaires are completed, the researcher will review compiled data. Students who do not have test scores available will be eliminated from the study.

The participating students' ISTEP writing scores will be reviewed and entered into the spreadsheet. Because the study is using tests from the previous school year, tests scores will already be available. Using ex post facto data will enable the research process to progress more quickly because there will be no need to wait four to six months on scored testing data to be returned.

The list of participants will be given to the school data coach. The data coach will use the school information system, Power School, to identify each participant's eligibility for Free and Reduced Meals. Because identifying students' eligibility for Free and Reduced Meals is confidential information, the data coach will randomly assign each student a number. The data coach will keep the list of students and their identifier confidential by securing the information. Only the data coach will have access to this information. It is not to be released to anyone, including the researcher.

Students will be categorized as eligible or not eligible. This information will be indicated on the spreadsheet. The spreadsheet will be coded as 1, eligible, or 2, not eligible. All data will be compiled in a spreadsheet and analyzed using a multiple regression analysis in SPSS.

DATA ANALYSIS

The multiple regression analysis is the best method for analyzing this data because as inferential statistics, it can be used to predict whether the results can apply to future populations. A multiple linear regression analysis will be used to determine the correlation between a criterion variable and the predictor variables (Gall, Gall, & Borg, 2010).

In other words, the analysis will determine a correlation between the population of eligible Free and Reduced Meal students and noneligible students and students' text volume and ISTEP scores. According to Baron and Byrne (2005), multiple linear regression analysis is one of the most widely used analyses in the education field because of its ability to provide a wide range of information about relationships among variables. Multiple regression also speaks to the statistical significance of relationships between data (Baron & Byrne, 2005), which is an accurate approach when examining a correlational study.

The first step is to analyze the correlation between the ISTEP scores and student text frequency, or the strongest predictor and the criterion variable. In this case, the strongest predictor is the frequency of texting. This yields the multiple correlation coefficient (R), which will be the first predictor entered into the multiple regression. The second predictor entered would be the students' Free or Reduced Meal eligibility. These two predictor variables together produce a multiple correlation coefficient to illustrate the strength of the correlation.

A scatterplot provides a visual analysis of the assumption of homoscedasticity between the predicted dependent variable scores and the errors of prediction (Gall, Gall, & Borg, 2010, p. 359). The scatterplot will reveal a positive linear relationship, a negative linear relationship, or no relationship.

At first glance, outliers, or extreme scores, may be isolated from the data set. Tabachnick and Fidell (2007) described the difference between the obtained dependent variable and the predicted dependent variable scores. If there is a true correlation between texting and writing performance, these scores should be the same.

If the assumption is met, the data points on a scatterplot are clustered around a horizontal line. This reveals a positive relationship, meaning a correlation between texting frequency and student writing performance. In contrast, any systematic pattern of clustering of scores is considered a violation (Tabachnick & Fidell, 2007).

If data points are randomly scattered with no pattern or shape, then the assumption of homoscedasticity is met and we can conclude that the research shows no correlation between the variables.

Determining a correlation does not with certainty identify a cause-and-effect relationship. Limitations, both external and internal threats to research, exist beyond the researcher's control, which affect the results of the study or influence the behavior of the participants (Gall, Gall, & Borg, 2010).

Possible limitations may be that the population of the participating middle school has a high poverty rate and consistently low standardized test scores. The findings in this setting may be different than findings at an affluent middle school with higher standardized test scores. An external threat and potential influence to the study is the limited data collected. A seven-day sample of texting behavior will not produce as accurate results as a sample which covers a longer period of time. Furthermore, the ISTEP scores used as the baseline to determine students' writing performance are one year old and may not accurately reflect students' current writing abilities.

An issue that perpetually poses a threat to the validity of any test is the test taker's level of motivation at the time the test is taken. Students may not attend to the assessment to the best of their ability, therefore skewing the data with inaccurate scores. Additionally, students utilize textspeak in a variety of social media, including Facebook and instant messaging. This study looks at only text messaging, one of many digital language platforms.

To address these threats, a future study could be replicated with a contrasting setting and demographic to verify that the results can be applied to a larger population and not just a high-poverty demographic. In addition, the survey that was used to collect data on student texting habits was validated through an organized review of content to ensure that questions were clear and interpreted clearly.

The survey provides information about student texting over a one-week period to better summarize overall texting behavior. Furthermore, once the current year's assessment data is released, it could be applied to the study in place of the dated testing scores. Furthermore, if the study is to be replicated, the researcher may consider including the participants' volume of messages sent through Facebook and instant messaging.

RESULTS

Text messaging has become an increasingly common form of communication, especially for adolescents (Varnhagen et al., 2009). Text messaging frequently uses "textspeak," which is characterized by the use of abbreviations, intentional misspellings, and improper grammar.

Although parents and teachers worry about the effect textspeak has on children's literacy (Cingel & Sundar, 2012), some studies have suggested that students benefit from textspeak, showing that those who are proficient in translating textspeak into proper English exhibit greater reading and language scores (Plester et al., 2009). The most common view, however, is that textspeak damages the formal writing skills of students (Thurlow, 2006).

The purpose of this study was to investigate the effect of texting on middle school students' formal writing achievement. This chapter begins with a description of the participants' sample characteristics. This is followed by a summary of the results along with a detailed analysis of the results. A brief summary concludes this chapter.

Descriptive Statistics

The final sample of sixty-three students consisted of thirty-eight (60.3 percent) girls and twenty-five (39.7 percent) boys. Most students were from the sixth grade ($n = 30$, 47.6 perent), with the remaining students almost equally split between the seventh ($n = 15$, 23.8 percent) and eighth grades ($n = 18$, 28.6 percent). Of the sixth-grade students, 53.3 percent were girls, and 46.7 percent were boys. Of the seventh-grade students, 66.7 percent were girls, and 33.3 percent were boys. These percentages were the same for eighth-grade students, of which 66.7 percent were girls, and 33.3 percent were boys.

The majority of students were eligible to receive free meals ($n = 44$, 69.8 percent). There were five students (7.9 percent) who received a reduced price meal, and 14 (22.2 percent) who received paid meals. In the sixth grade, 73.3 percent of students received a free meal, 13.3 percent of students received a reduced price meal, and 13.3 percent of students received a paid meal. There were no seventh-graders who received a reduced price meal; 53.3 percent of seventh-graders received a free meal, and 46.7 percent of students received a paid meal. There was only one eighth-grader in the sample who received a reduced price meal, 77.8 percent received a free meal, and 16.7 percent received a paid meal.

The highest proportion of students passed the ISTEP without high achievement ($n = 31$, 49.2 percent), with twenty-seven students failing (42.9 percent) and five students earning a high achievement pass (7.9 percent). Forty percent of sixth-graders passed without high achievement, 50.0 percent failed, and 10.0 percent passed with high achievement. A slight majority (53.3 percent) of seventh-graders also passed without high achievement, 40.0 percent failed, and 6.7 percent passed with high achievement. Of the eighth-graders, 61.1 percent passed without high achievement, 33.3 percent failed, and 5.6 percent passed with high achievement.

The average ISTEP score was 503.16 ($SD = 53.64$). In the sixth grade, the average ISTEP score was 482.467 ($SD = 40.04$). In the seventh grade, the average was 512.20 ($SD = 70.79$), and eighth-graders scored an average of 530.11 ($SD = 45.12$). The average number of texts sent by the students in the last week was 119.56 ($SD = 204.68$). Average number of text messages increased by grade level: eighth-graders sent the most texts on average ($M = 211.17$, $SD = 312.38$), seventh-graders sent an average of 129.9 ($SD = 181.27$), and sixth-graders had an average of 59.43 ($SD = 86.61$) sent.

Summary of the Results

One linear regression and one multiple linear regression were conducted, with frequency of texting and free/reduced meal eligibility predicting ISTEP performance scores. The results of these regressions were not significant, as indicated by p values less than 0.05 ($F(1, 61) = 1.84$, $p = 0.180$; $F(2, 60) = 1.19$, $p = 0.311$; Field, 2013). This suggests that text message frequency and free/reduced meal eligibility do not significantly predict ISTEP performance scores. As such, the null hypotheses for RQ1 and RQ2 cannot be rejected.

Detailed Analysis

RQ1. Is there a statistically significant relationship between frequency of texting and adolescent writing achievement?

H01. There is no correlation between the frequency of text messages sent each week and the writing achievement of middle school students.

This research question was examined using a simple linear regression. This is the appropriate analysis to perform when the researcher seeks to assess how a single predictor variable predicts a single criterion variable

(Field, 2013). In this case, the predictor variable corresponds to frequency of texting, and the criterion variable corresponds to adolescent writing achievement.

Prior to the analysis, the assumptions of the linear regression were assessed. The assumptions of linearity and homoscedasticity were assessed using a scatterplot of the residuals. Linearity assumes a linear (straight) relationship between the predictor and criterion variables and is assumed when a straight line is best fit through a scatterplot rather than a curved line (Tabachnick & Fidell, 2014).

Homoscedasticity assumes that scores appear in a block shape, with no major trend or pattern, indicating that scores are generally evenly distributed about the regression line (Tabachnick & Fidell, 2014). Visual examination of the scatterplot revealed that the assumption of linearity was met but that the assumption of homoscedasticity was not met because there is a classic cone-shaped pattern that indicates heteroscedasticity (Tabachnick & Fidell, 2014).

The overall regression equation was not significant, $F(1, 61) = 1.84$, $p = 0.180$. This indicates that text message frequency does not significantly predict ISTEP performance scores. As such, the null hypothesis cannot be rejected.

RQ2. Is there a statistically significant difference in the effect of texting between adolescents eligible for free/reduced meals and those who aren't?

H02. There is no difference in the effect of texting on middle school students eligible for Free and Reduced Meals and students who are not eligible.

To address this research question, a multiple linear regression was performed. The multiple linear regression is used when the predictive relationship between multiple predictor variables and one criterion variable is sought (Field, 2013). In this analysis, the predictor variables correspond to text message frequency and free/reduced meal eligibility.

The criterion variable corresponds to ISTEP performance scores. Prior to the analysis, the assumptions of the multiple linear regression—linearity and homoscedasticity—were examined using a scatterplot of the residuals. The assumption of linearity was met because the line of best fit is linear, and the assumption of homoscedasticity was not met because there is not a block-like, evenly distributed pattern (Tabachnick & Fidell, 2014).

The overall regression equation for this model was not significant, $F(2, 60) = 1.19$, $p = 0.311$. This suggests that the combined variables of text message frequency and free/reduced meal eligibility do not significantly predict ISTEP performance. As such, the individual predictors were not examined further. The null hypothesis cannot be rejected.

This study detailed the sample characteristics and analysis of the research questions. The sample consisted mostly of girls and mostly students in the sixth grade, with the rest of the sample almost evenly split between seventh- and eighth-graders. The majority were eligible for free meals, and most passed the ISTEP with high achievement. Students in the sixth grade tended to text the least and had the lowest average ISTEP scores, and eighth-graders tended to text the most and had the highest average ISTEP scores.

One simple linear regression and one multiple linear regression were conducted and were found not to be significant. These results suggested that neither text message frequency nor the combined model using text message frequency and free/reduced meal eligibility significantly predicted ISTEP score performance. As such, neither the null hypothesis for RQ1 nor the null hypothesis for RQ2 may be rejected.

DISCUSSION, CONCLUSIONS, AND RECOMMENDATIONS

The purpose of this study is to determine whether there was a correlation between middle school student writing achievement and the frequency of texting. The study began with the null hypothesis that there is no correlation between the frequency of text messages sent and the writing achievement of middle school students. The results verified the null hypothesis.

Previous studies have concluded that elementary students who have the ability to code-switch and use textspeak score higher in reading and spelling assessments. The assumption is that a student must have a solid grasp of language structure, phonics, and spelling to manipulate language as used in textspeak as addressed in the studies by Coe and Oakhill (2011), Plester et al. (2008), and Rosen et al. (2010).

The majority of research has been conducted with college undergraduates. Research found that college students appear to understand the appropriate utilization of textspeak and utilize it only in a casual context; by this point in their educational career and with their life experience, they understand when to use textspeak and when to use Standard English (Shafie et al., 2010). They typically do not use it when corresponding in a professional setting, with a superior, or in an academic context.

The major gap in research occurs at the adolescent level. There are few studies with concluding results on the effect of texting on adolescent students. The intent of this study was to help fill that gap.

SUMMARY OF FINDINGS

The study investigated the null hypothesis that there is no difference in the effect of texting on middle school students eligible for Free and Reduced Meals and students who are not eligible. This was verified. The analysis of results indicated that text message frequency and free/reduced meal eligibility did not significantly predict ISTEP score performance. Therefore, this test determined that there is no correlation between how often middle school students text and their writing achievement.

DISCUSSION

Because 78 percent of the sixty-three participants were identified as living in poverty, the postulation was they would be more susceptible to a negative influence of textspeak and be more likely to use it in academic work. Jensen's work on *Teaching with Poverty in Mind: What Being Poor Does to Kids' Brains and What Schools Can Do about It* (2009) concludes that students who live in poverty have underdeveloped cognitive skills and executive function. He states, "Socioeconomic status is strongly associated with a number of indices of children's cognitive ability, including IQ, achievement tests, grade retention rates, and literacy" (p. 31).

This association is established from birth through adolescence and into adulthood. Because of the preceding factors, these students attain lower academic achievement and score lower on examinations. Testing bias may also occur, which is another detriment to students who do not have the same background knowledge and norms of middle-class test writers. Executive function affects a student's ability to react appropriately in a specific environment, like talking out of turn and waiting in line. If a student is deficient in this area, success in an educational institution is highly unlikely.

Earlier work done by Crystal (2008), Bloom (2010), Coe and Oakhill (2011), Plester et al. (2008), and Rosen et al. (2010) indicated that elementary-aged students perform higher in the areas of literacy if they have been exposed to texting. Elementary students who text can also spell phonetically, which demonstrates phonemic awareness. They can manipulate language to craft phrases, which exhibits an understanding of syntax and structure. To use textspeak, one must have an advanced understanding of language, spelling, and communicative writing, all essential components of first-class writing.

Texting studies have been done on undergraduate students more than any other age group (e.g., Kemp & Bushnell, 2011; Drouin, 2011; Grace et al., 2013; Kemp, 2010; Lewis & Fabos, 2005; Powell & Dixon, 2011; Yousaf & Ahmed, 2013). These studies covered a variety of issues concerning texting, from preferred methods of communication to the amount of textspeak used in correspondence with professors. The studies concluded that the majority of US and foreign undergraduate college students are not falling prey to textspeak in academic writing. Only 13 to 16 percent of students used missing punctuation or capitalization in professional correspondence (DeJong & Kemp, 2010).

However, this study was conducted to fill the gap of empirical data on adolescents and textspeak. If textspeak is the demise of the English language, educators may be the first to uncover the evidence in classroom writing. Little to no research has been conducted on how the frequency of textspeak affects writing performance in middle school students, which is interesting because this group sends nearly two hundred text messages a day.

The results of this study did not support the popular hypothesis. The data showed that out of the sixty-three participating students, 49 percent of students passed the state writing exam and 43 percent failed. There was no correlation between texting and whether students passed or failed the state standardized writing exam. Therefore, the frequency of texting does not harm student test scores. Nor does the amount of student textspeak contribute to phenomenal writing skills.

Research has proven that children who use textspeak tend to do better in academic writing, spelling, and language arts. We also know that by the time students reach college, the majority of the time they know when to use formal or casual language registers whether it's in speaking or writing. Questions still remain, however, whether middle school students' writing skills are affected by texting habits.

IMPLICATIONS

Educators measure excellence in writing by correct spelling, word counts, and age-appropriate vocabulary. Linguists have uncovered a truth that most educators have not, and that is that language is interaction. Textspeak, a written form of language, demonstrates the results of interaction within a subculture just as dialect is considered interaction within a sociocultural group (Blum, 2010). To evaluate student writing, educators have limited language to quantify its value and grade the effect of expression.

As technology continuously changes, communication styles will most likely change too. Teachers are encouraged to adopt a new perspective of language: language as interaction and language as a process of trial and error. All speakers are language learners. We continue to learn new vocabulary, develop various dialects, and learn new rules, depending on our changing social setting.

Code-switching is the skill of transitioning back and forth between formal and casual registers of language, depending on context and setting. In a technology-driven environment, the line can become blurred in an online academic setting (Hawley Turner & Hicks, 2011). Teachers may have to give explicit instructions about the type of language that is appropriate to use in discussion board forums or online communications between classmates.

Especially as more schools are moving to a one-to-one initiative, meaning each student is equipped with a laptop or tablet, the majority of their academic work is now being housed in the same platform used for their entertainment and social exchanges.

Negotiating the code, or allowing students to help decide what rules of language will be followed during certain class activities, can assist teachers in adopting a new, flexible attitude toward language. Permitting students to journal or brainstorm in textspeak, because it's the code that comes most naturally to them (Varnhagen et al., 2009), can aid their thinking and ultimately support their writing. Teachers may model their journey toward digital literacy by reading and responding to educational blogs, increasing their social media networks, and contributing to educational forums.

As educators we have a responsibility to teach our students to succeed in a quickly changing, digital world. Students must become digital writers and citizens so they can contribute to the larger society of which they are part. "In the spirit of social justice, we believe that digital literacy is an emerging human right and that it is vital for community development and citizenship" (Hawley Turner & Hicks, 2011).

LIMITATIONS

One possible limitation for the study is collecting data from only a one-week period of time. Analyzing text message frequency over a one-month period of time may have provided a better window into students' texting habits and behaviors. Furthermore, a more reliable system for counting text messages would have been better than students manually going through their text messages and counting each sent text from each contact. There is a lot of room for error in asking students, who may not be paying careful attention, to give an exact count of messages. Some students could have easily counted erroneously or counted both sent and received text messages instead of only sent messages.

Another limitation to the study was the number of participants. Sixty-three participants were the minimum needed for a credible study. Unfortunately, of the three hundred students who received parent permission to participate in the study, only 101 students completed the online survey. Of the 101 students who completed the online survey, there were thirty-eight students who did not have a personal cell phone or did not have ISTEP scores available, leaving a total of sixty-three student participants.

Forty-eight percent of the participating students were sixth-graders, 26 percent were seventh-graders, and 28 percent were eighth-graders. It would have been better to have a more even distribution of each grade represented. I believe it may have provided more accurate data to have more eighth-grade participants in the study. Eighth-graders are more likely to have a cell phone than are sixth-graders and more likely to have developed stronger texting behaviors by age thirteen rather than age eleven.

Demographics may have indirectly created bias in the results of the study. Because 78 percent of Highland Middle School students live in poverty, the average state test scores run lower than school districts that are primarily made up of middle-class students. This study may provide different findings if it were conducted in a different demographic context.

RECOMMENDATIONS FOR FUTURE RESEARCH

Future research should be conducted in a similar manner but with a greater number of participants aged twelve and thirteen years. If the study were replicated, it would be more advantageous to subscribe a more accurate method for collecting the frequency of text messaging, such as using an app on each participant's phone that would provide the exact number of sent text messages.

Participants could download the app once they had consented to participate and begin immediate use. The app could then report the number of texts sent directly to the researcher at the end of a recorded period. This wouldn't infringe on privacy of participants or allow for participant error in counting.

It may be advantageous to collect data from a longer texting period and record a broader sample of student writing scores instead of looking at a single standardized test. In many cases, participants had to be eliminated from the study because they did not have scores to report. Looking at students' writing portfolios and examining select pieces would give a more representative sample of students' writing performance.

Because the study was conducted in a population of high-poverty students, it would be interesting to see whether the results differ in a population of middle-class as well as affluent middle school students.

SUMMARY

Texting burst into Western culture. It changed human behavior and is leaving behind a lasting imprint on the Standard English language. Individuals sharing a common tongue form a connected culture, and textspeak has further bonded society through the English language. Textspeak has permeated Standard English and made phrases such as "lol, ttyl, idk" ubiquitous terminology for children, teens, and adults. Accounts of textspeak gone wrong are told as humorous anecdotes.

"Your great aunt passed away. LOL"

"Why is that funny?"

"It's not funny, why would you say that?"

"Mom, LOL means laughing out loud."

"Oh no! I just sent that to everyone! I thought it meant lots of love!"

Texting has the ability to disguise our deficiencies through the magic of autocorrect. Now that everyone has the same spelling capabilities, content becomes king over conventions. Writers are free to explore ideas, cohesion of thoughts, and structure of verse, all skills one may argue that are more significant than attention to primeval rules, such as *i* before *e*. Textspeak has the power to communicate more cleverly and to display personality and tone through emojis and to add another dimension to writing.

All of the wonders of texting, yet educators are still concerned that it is the degeneration of student writing. The primary platform adolescents use to communicate is texting. Teens send approximately 3,500 text messages every month, almost twice as any other age group (Cingel & Sundar, 2012). Eighty-one percent of middle school teachers believe textspeak has negative effects on student writing, commenting that many students use emoticons, acronyms, and shortened phonetic spelling in their school writing assignments. This study set out to support those teachers' theories; however, the results concluded something different.

Textspeak Glossary

*$	Starbucks
10Q	thank you
121	one to one
143	I love you
1432	I love you too
14AA41	one for all and all for one
1daful	wonderful
2	to, too, two
20	location
247	24 hours a day, 7 days a week, all the time
2b	to be
2BZ4UQT	too busy for you cutey
2day	today
2moro	tomorrow
2nite	tonight
2QT	too cute
303	mom
4	for, four
411	information
459	I love you

4COL	for crying out loud
4eva/4ever	forever
<3	heart, love
@	at
ab/abt	about
ab2/abt2	about to
add	address
B4	before
BC	because
BIBI	bye bye
BTW	by the way
BRO	be right over
chilaxn	chilling, relaxing
CM	call me
CMU	crack me up
coo	cool
CP	sleepy
CUL8R	see you later
cuz	because
cya	see you
D	there
D8	date
def	definitely
DINR	dinner
DK	don't know
DMI	don't mention it
doin	doing
DYAC	darn you autocorrect
E123	easy as 1, 2, 3
EMA	email address
EML	email me later
EVRY1	everyone

Textspeak Glossary

EZ	easy
F2C	failure to communicate
F2F	face-to-face, Facetime
F	friend
FAV	favorite
FIFO	first in, first out
FOMC	falling off my chair
FOMO	fear of missing out
FSR	for some reason
FTBL	football
FWD	forward
FYEO	for your eyes only
FYI	for your information
G1	good one
G2G	good to go
g98t	goodnight
GF	girlfriend
GI	Google it
gratz	congratulations
GR8	great
H8	hate
H&K	hugs and kisses
hahaha	laughing
HAND	have a nice day
hv	have
Hi5	high five
h/o	hold on
howru	How are you?
hx	hospital
I 1DR	I wonder
I <3 U	I love you
IAW	I agree with

ID1OT	idiot
IDK	I don't know
IDKU	I don't know you
IHNC	I have no clue
IMRU	I am, are you?
IOW	in other words
IRL	in real life
ITA	I totally agree
ITZAD8	it's a date
J/C	just checking
jealz	jealous
JIC	just in case
JK	just kidding
J4F	just for fun
kewl	cool
KIT	keep in touch
L8tR	later
L@U	laughing at you
LFTI	looking forward to it
LOL	laughing out loud
LOLZ	lots of laughs
LUMU	love you, miss you
LY4E	love you forever
LYL	love you lots
M4C	meet for coffee
mlm	giving the digital middle finger
mwah	kissing sound
MYOB	mind your own business
newayz	anyways
ne1	anyone
Ne2H	need to have
NNWW	nudge, nudge, wink, wink

NP	no problem
NQA	no questions asked
nthn	nothing
nvm	nevermind
ofc	of course
OIC	oh, I see
OMG	oh my goodness
OMIK	open mouth, insert keyboard
OMW	on my way
OOAK	one of a kind
OT	off topic
OTL	out to lunch
OTR	on the road
ova	over
PZA	pizza
P3r50N	person
PCM	please call me
peeps	people
PLS	please
PPL	people
puter	computer
qix	quick
QT	quiet
r	are
r u?	are you
r u da?	Are you there?
r u goin?	Are you going?
REHI	hi again
rgds	regards
RIYL	recommend if you like
RN	right now
RNY	rainy

ROFL	rolling on the floor laughing
ROFLOL	rolling on the floor laughing out loud
RUSOS	Are you in trouble?
RUT	Are you there?
RU^	Are you up?
S^	What's up?
sm1	someone
sthg	something
SoIC	so I see
soz	sorry
srsly	seriously
sry	sorry
STR8	straight
STW	search the web
sup	What's up?
sux	sucks
SWAK	sealed with a kiss
sweet<3	sweetheart
t+	think positive
t2go	time to go
T2UL	talk to you later
T@UL	talk at you later
TBC	to be continued
TFX	traffic
TMI	too much information
TOY	thinking of you
troo	true
TTS	text to speech
TTYL	talk to you later
TTYL8R	talk to you later
TWTR	Twitter
TXT MSG	text message

TYVM	thank you very much
U2?	You too?
UDH82BME	you'd hate to be me
UNOIT	you know it
ur	you are
URZ	yours
W/E	weekend
W8	wait
W@	what
wan2	want to
wk	week
wru	Where are you?
W2Go	way to go
wuz	was
WWW	World Wide Web
X	times
XI10	exciting
XOXO	hugs and kisses
XOXOZZZ	hugs and kisses and sweet dreams
Y	Why?
ya	yes
YF	wife
YOLO	you only live once
Z	said
ZZZ	sleeping, bored

References

Adler, R., & Proctor, R. (2014). *Looking out, looking in* (14th ed.). Boston, MA: Cengage Learning Publishing.
Allred, R. (1977). *Spelling: The application of research findings*. Washington, DC: National Education Association.
Anderson, R. I. (1981). Research in shorthand and transcription. *Journal of Business Education, 57*(2), 75–78.
Androutsopoulos, J. (2008). Non-standard spellings in media texts: The case of German fanzines. *Journal of Sociolinguistics, 44*, 514–533.
Apple. (2016). Dillan's Voice. Retrieved from: https://www.youtube.com/watch?v=oMN2PeFama0&feature=youtu.be.
Araque, J., Maiden, R., Bravo, N., Estrada, I., Evans, K., Hubchik, K., Kirby, K., Reddy, M. (2013). Computer usage and access in low-income urban communities. *Computers in Human Behavior, 29*(4), 1393–1401. doi:10.1016/j.chb.2013.01.032.
Baron, N. (2005). Instant messaging and the future of language. *Communications of the ACM, 48*(7), 29–31.
Baron, N. (2009). Are digital media changing language? *Educational Leadership, 66*(6), 42–46.
Baron, R., & Byrne, D. (2005). *Social Psychology: Understanding Human Interaction* (7th Ed.). Boston: Pearson.
Beeson, P., Higginson, K., & Rising, K. (2013). Writing treatment for aphasia: A texting approach. *Journal of Speech, Language, and Hearing Research, 56*(3), 945.
Berninger, V. W., Vaughan, K., Abbott, R. D., Brooks, A., Begay, K., Curtin, G., Byrd, K., & Graham, S. (2000). Language-based spelling instruction: Teaching children to make multiple connections between spoken and written words. *Learning Disability Quarterly, 23*(2), 117–135.
Blum, S. (2010). *My Word! Plagiarism and College Culture*. New York: Cornell University Press.
Boone, W. J., & Scantlebury, K. (2006). The role of Rasch analysis when conducting science education research utilizing multiple-choice tests. *Science Education, 90*(2), 253–269.
Brice Heath, S. (1999). *Ways with words: Language, life, and work in communities and classrooms*. Cambridge, MA: Cambridge University Press.
Brignall, T. W., & Van Valey, T. (2005). The impact of Internet communications on social interaction. *Sociological Spectrum, 25*(3), 335–348.
Brimi, H. (2011). Reliability of grading high school work in English. *Practical Assessment, Research & Evaluation, 16*(17), 1–12.

British Council Lesson Plan: Texting [PDF document]. Retrieved from British Council Online website: https://www.teachingenglish.org.uk/sites/teacheng/files/Texting_plan.pdf.

Cingel, D., & Sundar, D. (2012). Texting, techspeak, and tweens: The relationship between text messaging and English grammar skills. *New Media Society, 14*(8), 1304–1320.

Coe, J. E. L., & Oakhill, J. V. (2011). "txtn is ez f u no h2 rd": The relationship between reading ability and text messaging behavior. *Journal of Computer Assisted Learning, 27*, 4–17. doi:10.1111/j.1365-2729.2100.00404.x.

Cohen, J. (1992). A power primer. *Psychological Bulletin, 112*(1), 155.

Conley, D. (2008). *College Knowledge: What it Really Takes for Students to Succeed and What We Can Do to Get Them Ready*. San Francisco: Jossey-Bass.

Connective Writing. (n.d.). Will Richardson's Wiki. Retrieved from http://weblogged.wikispaces.com/Connective+Writing.

Crystal, D. (2008). *Txtng: The gr8 db8*. New York: Oxford University Press.

Danesi, M. (2009). Explaining change in language: A cybersemiotic perspective. *Entropy, 11*(4), 1055–1072.

Dansieh, S. (2011). SMS texting and its potential impacts on students' written communication skills. *International Journal of English Linguistics, 1*(2), 222–229.

Davis, S. L. (2004). *Predicting exceptionality, student achievement, and ISTEP scores using pre-school screening scores of Amish and English children*. (Doctoral dissertation). Retrieved from http://liblink.bsu.edu/catkey/1301630.

DeGennaro, D. (2005). Should we ban instant messaging in school? *Learning & Leading with Technology, 32*(7), 6.

Deumert, A., & Lexander, K. (2013). Texting Africa: Writing as performance. *Journal of Sociolinguistics, 17*(4), 522–546.

Deutscher, G. (2005). *The Unfolding of Language: An Evolutionary Tour of Mankind's Greatest Invention*. New York: Henry Holt and Company.

Devitt, A. (1993). Generalizing about genre: New conceptualizations of an old concept. *College Composition and Communication, 44*, 573–586.

de Winter, J. C. F. (2013). Using the Student's *t*-test with extremely small sample sizes. *Practical Assessment, Research & Evaluation, 18*(10), 1–12.

Dixon, H. (2011). Texting, tweeting, and other Internet abbreviations. *Judges Journal, 50*(4), 30.

Drago, E. (2015). The effect of technology on face-to-face communication. *The Elon Journal of Undergraduate Research in Communications, 6*(1), 13–19.

Drouin, M. A. (2011). College students' text messaging, use of textese and literacy skills. *Journal of Computer Assisted Learning, 27*(1), 67–75.

Drouin, M., & Driver, B. (2014). Texting, textese and literacy abilities: A naturalistic study. *Journal of Research in Reading, 37*(3), 250–267. doi:10.1111/j.1467-9817.2012.01532.x.

Durken, K., Conti-Ramsden, G., & Walker, A. J. (2011). Txt lang: Texting, textism use and literacy abilities in adolescents with and without specific language impairment. *Journal of Computer Assisted Learning, 27*(1), 49–57.

Ehri, L. (2000). Learning to read and learning to spell: Two sides of a coin. *Topics in Language Disorders, 20*(3), 19–49.

Faul, F., Erdfelder, E., Lang, A. G., & Buchner, A. (2007). G*Power 3: A flexible statistical power analysis program for the social, behavioral, and biomedical sciences. *Behavior Research Methods, 39*(2), 175–191.

Fay, J., & Funk, D. (2010). *Teaching with Love & Logic: Taking Control of the Classroom*. Golden, CO: Love & Logic Institute.

Fishman, J., Lunsford, A., McGregor, B., & Otuteye, M. (2005). Performing writing, performing literacy. *College Composition and Communication, 57*(2), 224–252.

Fitts, D. A. (2010). Improved stopping rules for the design of efficient small-sample experiments in biomedical and biobehavioral research. *Behavior Research Methods, 42*, 3–22.

Fitzgerald, J. (1951). *The teaching of spelling*. Milwaukee: Bruce Publishing Company.

Flower, L., & Hayes, J. R. (1981). A cognitive process theory of writing. *College Composition and Communication, 32*(4), 365–387. doi:10.2307/356600.

Forrester, M. (1993, May). Development of Young Children's Social-Cognitive Skills. [Book review]. *Journal of Child Psychology & Psychiatry & Allied Disciplines, 34*(4), 605–606.
Frey, N., & Fisher, D. (2008). Doing the right thing with technology. *The English Journal, 97*(6), 38–42.
Fry, E. B., Fountoukidis, D. L., & Kress, J. E. (2000). *The reading teacher's book of lists* (4th ed.). San Francisco, CA: Jossey-Bass.
Gall, J., Gall, M., & Borg, W. (2006). *Educational Research: An Introduction (8th Ed.)*. New York: Pearson.
Gee, J. P. 2003. *What video games have to teach us about learning and literacy*. New York: Palgrave Macmillan.
Grace, A., Kemp, N., Martin, F. H., & Parrila, R. (2013). Undergraduates' text messaging language and literacy skills. *Reading and Writing, 27*(5), 855–873. doi:10.1007/s11145-013-9471-2.
Graham, S. (1999). Handwriting and spelling instruction for students with learning disabilities: A review. *Learning Disability Quarterly, 22*(2), 78–98.
Graham, S., & Hebert, M. (2010). *Writing to read: Evidence for how writing can improve reading*. Washington, DC: Alliance for Excellent Education.
Haas, C., & Takayoshi, P. (2011). Young people's everyday literacies: The language features of instant messaging. *Research in the Teaching of English, 45*(4), 378–405.
Harley, D., Winn, S., Pemberton, S., & Wilcox, P. (2007). Using texting to support students' transition to university. *Innovations in Education and Teaching International, 44*(3), 229–241.
Hawley Turner, K., & Hicks, T. (2011). "That's not writing": Exploring the intersection of digital writing, community literacy, and social justice. *Community Literacy Journal, 6*(1), 55–78.
Hekin, R., Harmon, J., Pate, E., & Moorman, H. (2008, March). Spelling it right: Heading in the right direction. *Voices from the Middle, 15*(3), 7.
Hicks, T., & Hawley Turner, K. (2013). No longer a luxury: Digital literacy can't wait. *English Journal, 102*(6), 58–65.
Horn, E. (1926). *A Basic Vocabulary of 10,000 Words Most Commonly Used in Writing*. Iowa City: University of Iowa.
Horn, T., & Otto, H. (1954). *Spelling Instruction: A Curriculum-Wide Approach*. Austin: University of Texas.
How to Handle Misbehaving Students: "Maintaining Classroom Discipline." 1947 McGraw-Hill Films (1947). Retrieved from: https://www.youtube.com/watch?v=zDoflTceN2w.
Huitt, W. (2011). Bloom et al.'s Taxonomy of the Cognitive Domain. Retrieved from www.edpsycinteractive.org/topics/cognition/bloom.html.
Jensen, E. (2009). *Teaching with poverty in mind: What being poor does to kids' brains and what schools can do about it*. Alexandria, VA: ASCD.
Kemp, N. (2010). Texting vs. txting: Efficiency in reading and writing text messages, and links with other linguistic skills. *Writing Systems Research, 2*, 53–71.
Kemp, N., & Bushnell, C. (2011). Children's text messaging: Input methods and links with literacy. *Journal of Computer Assisted Learning, 27*(1), 18–27.
Kemp, N., Wood, C., & Waldron, S. (2014). Do I Know It's Wrong: Children's and Adults' Use of Unconventional Grammar in Text Messaging. *Reading and Writing: An Interdisciplinary Journal 27*(9), 1585–1602.
Kolodziej, N., & Columba, L. (2005). Inventive spelling: Guidelines for parents. *Reading Improvement, 42*(4), 212–223.
Kopkowski, C. (2008, April). Why they leave: Lack of respect, NCLB, and underfunding—in a topsy-turvy profession, what can make today's teachers stay? Retrieved from www.nea.org/archive/12630.htm.
Lankshear, C., & Knobel, M. (2002). Do we have your attention? New literacies, digital technologies, and the education of adolescents. *Adolescents and Literacies in a Digital World, 11*, 19–39.

Leathwood, C. (2001). *The road to independence? Policy, pedagogy and "die independent learner" in higher education.* Paper presented at the 31st SCUTREA Conference. Retrieved from www.leeds.ac.uk.ezproxy.liberty.edu:2048/educol/documents/00002491.htm.

Lenhart, A., Arafeh, S., Smith, A., & Macgill, A. (2008). Writing, technology and teens. Retrieved from www.pewinternet.org/Reports/2008/Writing-Technology.

Lewin, T. (2008, April 25). Informal style of text messages is showing up in schoolwork. *New York Times.* Retrieved from www.nytimes.com/2008/04/25/education/25writing.html.

Lewis, C. & Fabos, B. (2005). Instant messaging, literacies, and social identities. *Reading Research Quarterly, 40*(4), 470–501. doi:10.1598/rrq.40.4.5.

MacKenzie-Hoy, T. (2006). "Textese" has been around for years. Retrieved from www.engineeringnews.co.za/article.php?a_id=85379.

Mahiri, J., & Wright, D. (2012). Literacy learning within community action projects for social change. *Journal of Adolescent & Adult Literacy, 56*(2), 123–131.

Mehta, P. D., Foorman, B. R., Branum-Martin, L., & Taylor, W. P. (2005). Literacy as a unidimensional multilevel construct: Validation, sources of influence, and implications in a longitudinal study in grades 1 to 4. *Scientific Studies of Reading, 9*(2), 85–116.

Milian, M. (2009, May 3). Why text messages are limited to 160 characters. *Los Angeles Times.* Retrieved from http://latimesblogs.latimes.com/technology/2009/05/invented-text-messaging.html.

Misra, S., Cheng, L., Genevie, J., & Yuan, M. (2014). The iPhone effect: The quality of in-person social interactions in the presence of mobile devices. *Environment and Behavior, 48*(2), 1–24.

Missall, K., Mercer, S., Martinez, R., & Casebeer, D. (2012). Concurrent and longitudinal patterns and trends in performance on early numeracy curriculum-based measures in kindergarten through third grade. *Assessment for Effective Intervention, 37*(2), 95–106.

Moats, L., & Dakin, K. (2008). *Basic Facts about Dyslexia and other Reading Problems.* Baltimore, MD: International Dyslexia Association.

Monson, J. (1975). Is spelling spelled rut, routine, or revitalized? *Elementary English,* 52, 223–224.

Montgomery, D. J., Karlan, G. R., and Coutinho, M. (2001). The effectiveness of word processor spell checker programs to produce target words for misspellings generated by students with learning disabilities. *Journal of Special Education Technology, 16*(2), 27–41.

Newman, F., & Holzman, L. (2014). *Lev Vygotsky: Revolutionary scientist.* New York: Psychology Press.

Ormrod, J. (2011). *Educational PsychologyL Developing Learners* (7th ed.). Hudson, NY: Pearson Publishing.

Payne, R. K. (2005). *A Framework for Understanding Poverty* (4th rev. ed.). Highlands, TX: Aha! Process.

Pick, J., Sarkar, A., & Johnson, J. (2014). United States digital divide: State level analysis of spatial clustering and multivariate determinants of ICT utilization. *Socio-Economic Planning Sciences, 49,* 16–32. doi:10.1016/j.seps.2014.09.001

Plester, B., Wood, C., & Bell, V. (2008). Txt msg n school literacy: Does texting and knowledge of text abbreviations adversely affect children's literacy attainment? *Literacy, 42*(3), 137–144.

Plester, B., Wood, C., & Joshi, P. (2009). Exploring the relationship between children's knowledge of text message abbreviations and school literacy outcomes. *British Journal of Developmental Psychology, 27*(1), 145–161.

Powell, D., & Dixon, M. (2011). Does SMS text messaging help or harm adults' knowledge of standard spelling? *Journal of Computer Assisted Learning, 27,* 58–66. doi:10.1111/j.1365-2729.2010.00403.x.

Prensky, M. (2001). Digital natives, digital immigrants. Retrieved from http://marcprensky.com/writing/Prensky%20-%20Digital%20Natives,%20Digital%20Immigrants%20-%20Part1.pdf.

Prescott, A., & Simpson, E. (2004). Effective student motivation commences with resolving "dissatisfiers." *Journal of Further and Higher Education, 28*(3), 248–259.

References

Puentedura, R. (2006). Transformation, technology, and education. Blog post. Retrieved from http://hippasus.com/resources/tte/.

Purcell, K., Buchanan, J., & Friedrich, L. (2013). The impact of digital tools on student writing and how writing is taught in schools. *Pew Research National Writing Project*. Retrieved from: http://pewinternet.org/Reports/2013/Teachers-technology-and-writing.

Rideout, V. (2012). Children, teens, and entertainment media: A view from the classroom. Retrieved from www.commonsensemedia.org/research/children-teens-and-entertainment-media-the-view-from-the-classroom.

Rinsland, H. (1945). *A Basic Vocabulary of Elementary School Children*. New York: Macmillan.

Rosen, L. D. (2015, January 18). iPhone separation anxiety: It's real and it's not good for you. *Psychology Today*.

Rosen, L., Chang, J., Erwin, L., Carrier, L., & Cheever, N. (2010). The relationship between "textisms" and formal and informal writing among young adults. *Communication Research, 37*(3), 420–440. doi:10.1177/0093659219362465.

Separation Anxiety. (n.d.). Retrieved from https://www.psychologytoday.com/conditions/separation-anxiety.

Shafie, L., Azida, N., & Osman, N. (2010). SMS language and college writing: The languages of the college texters. *iJET, 5*(1), 26–31.

Shorthand. (n.d.). In *Encyclopedia Britannica online*. Retrieved from www.britannica.com/topic/shorthand.

Simoes-Perlant, A., Thibault, M. P., Lanchantin, T., Combes, C., Volckaert-Legrier, O., & Largy, P. (2012). How adolescents with dyslexia dysorthographia use texting. *Written Language & Literacy, 15*(1), 65–79.

Singer, B., & Bashir, A. (2004). Developmental variations in writing. *Handbook of Language and Literacy: Development and Disorders*. New York: Guilford.

Smagorinsky, P. (2007). *Vygotsky and Literary Research: A Methodological Framework (Practice of Research Method)*. Milford, CT: Sense Publishing.

Snow, C. E., Griffin, P., and Burns, M. S. (eds.) (2005). *Knowledge to Support the Teaching of Reading: Preparing Teachers for a Changing World*. San Francisco: Jossey-Bass.

Spatafora, J. N. (2012). IM learning 2 write? A study on how instant messaging shapes student writing. (Unpublished master's thesis). Queens University, Kingston, Ontario, Canada.

Swanson, H. L., Hoskyn, M., & Lee, C. (1999). *Interventions for Students with Learning Disabilities: A Meta-Analysis of Treatment Outcomes*. New York: Guilford Press.

Sweeny, S. M. (2010). Writing for the instant messaging and text messaging generation: Using new literacies to support writing instruction. *Journal of Adolescent & Adult Literacy, 54*(2), 121–130.

Tabachnick, B. G., & Fidell, L. S. (2007). *Using Multivariate Statistics (5th Ed.)*. New York: Allyn and Bacon.

Thurlow, C. (2006). From statistical panic to moral panic: The metadiscursive construction and popular exaggeration of new media language in the print media. *Journal of Computer-Mediated Communication, 7*(7), 667–701.

Turkle, S. (2012). *Alone together: Why we expect more from technology and less from each other*. New York: Basic Books.

Varnhagen, C., McFall, P., Pugh, N., Routledge, L., Sumida-MacDonald, H., & Kwong, T. (2009). Lol: New language and spelling in instant messaging. *Reading and Writing, 23*(6), 719–733. doi:10.1007/s11145-009-9181-y.

Veater, H., Plester, B., & Wood, C. (2010). Use of text message abbreviations and literacy skills in children with dyslexia. *Dyslexia, 17*(1), 65–71.

Vygotsky, L. (1930). *Mind and society: The prehistory of written language*. Cambridge, MA: Harvard University Press.

Warner, R. (2013). *Applied statistics* (2nd ed.). Thousand Oaks, CA: Sage Publishing.

Wheeler, R., & Swords, R. (2012). *Code-switching: Teaching Standard English in urban classrooms*. Urbana, IL: National Council of Teachers of English.

Wilde, S. (2008). "My kids can't spell and I don't want to deal with it": Spelling in middle school. *Voices from the Middle, 15*(3), 10–15.

Wilson, M. (2005). The changing discourse of language study. *English Journal, 90*(4), 31–37.
Wood, C., Jackson, E., & Hart, B. (2011). The effect of text messaging on 9- and 10-year-old children's reading, spelling, and phonological processing skills. *Journal of Computer Assisted Learning, 27,* 28–36.
Wormeli, R. (2006). *Fair isn't always equal: Assessing & grading in the differentiated classroom.* Portland, ME: Stenhouse Publishers.
Yousaf, A., & Ahmed, M. (2013). Effects of SMS on writing skills of the university students in Pakistan: A case study of Gujrat. *Asian Economic and Financial Review, 3*(3), 389–397.

About the Author

Jennifer French has served as an English teacher, an instructional coach, an assistant professor, and a school consultant. She is currently director of Curriculum, Instruction & Assessment for a school district in southern Indiana, where she lives with her husband, four children, and two corgis.

www.ingramcontent.com/pod-product-compliance
Lightning Source LLC
Chambersburg PA
CBHW032030230426
43671CB00005B/258